Aspects of modern sociology

The social structure of modern Britain

GENERAL EDITORS

John Barron Mays
Eleanor Rathbone, Professor of Sociology, University of Liverpool

Maurice Craft
Senior Lecturer in Education, University of Exeter

The Family

Mary Farmer

Lecturer in Social Science
University of Liverpool

Longman

LONGMAN GROUP LTD
London and Harlow

Associated companies, branches and representatives throughout the world

© *Longman Group Ltd* 1970

First published 1970
Fourth impression 1975

ISBN 0 582 48800.1 (Cased)
ISBN 0 582 48801.X (Paper)

Printed in Great Britain by
Lowe & Brydone (Printers) Ltd, Thetford, Norfolk

Contents

Editors' Preface

British higher education is now witnessing a very rapid expansion of teaching and research in the social sciences, and, in particular, in sociology. This new series has been designed for courses offered by universities, colleges of education, colleges of technology, and colleges of further education to meet the needs of students training for social work, teaching and a wide variety of other professions. It does not attempt a comprehensive treatment of the whole field of sociology, but concentrates on the social structure of modern Britain which forms a central feature of most university and college sociology courses in this country. Its purpose is to offer an analysis of our contemporary society through the study of basic demographic, ideological and structural features, and through the study of such major social institutions as the family, education, the economic and political structure, and so on.

The aim has been to produce a series of introductory texts which will in combination form the basis for a sustained course of study, but each volume has been designed as a single whole and can be read in its own right.

We hope that the topics covered in the series will prove attractive to a wide reading public and that, in addition to students, others who wish to know more than is readily available about the nature and structure of their own society will find them of interest.

JOHN BARRON MAYS
MAURICE CRAFT

Introduction

The prospect ahead

Thirty years ago, between the two wars, a summary of contemporary thinking on the sociological aspects of the family would have left the reader with the impression that here was a decaying, outworn institution, denuded of almost all its functions, visibly in the terminal stages of a protracted senility, its life tenuously prolonged by the reactionary attitudes of the more privileged social classes. The inference implicitly, and sometimes explicitly drawn, was that a helping hand to speed on the dying and cut short the death agonies would not be amiss. Few sociologists have been writing in such terms of late. It is true that certain traditional functions of the family such as education and social security have been transferred substantially to other agencies which, in a technological age, can now perform them with greater efficiency than the family. But it is also true that this supposedly moribund institution is proving extremely resilient, and the consensus of opinion among sociologists during the last decade or so has been that, not only is the family alive, but that it has proved capable of adapting itself and adjusting to meet the needs of a rapidly changing society and, indeed, that it is continuing to perform important functions strenuously and effectively. Ronald Fletcher summarises this point of view forcibly when he concludes that on the sociological evidence,

The family has *not* declined. The family is *not* less stable than hitherto. The standards of parenthood and parental responsibility have *not* deteriorated.

On the contrary, as he puts it later,

The family is now concerned with a more detailed and refined satisfaction of needs than hitherto, and it is more intimately and responsibly bound up with the wider and more complicated network of social institutions in the modern state than it was prior to industrialization.[1]

I

Thus for a time it appeared that the family, its temporary list corrected, could now sail full steam ahead, its captain and crew relaxing in a haze of self-congratulation. But parents did not enjoy their complacency for long.

Against a background of mounting restiveness among the 'pop' generation, whose challenge to the assumptions and edicts of all kinds of authority appeared more insistent than ever before, the family, as we know it, was subjected to a full-scale attack by Dr Edmund Leach in one of the 1967 Reith Lectures.[2] His theme was directed to the conclusion that the isolation and intimacy of family life incubates hate which finds expression in conflict in the wider community. Our society he described as 'a loose assemblage of isolated groups of parents and children' and summed up his views as follows:

In the past, kinsfolk and neighbours gave the individual continuous moral support throughout his life. Today the domestic household is isolated. The family looks inward upon itself; there is an intensification of emotional stress between husband and wife, and parents and children. The strain is greater than most of us can bear. Far from being the basis of the good society, the family, with its narrow privacy and tawdry secrets, is the source of all our discontents.

He went on, emphatically:

Our present society is emotionally very uncomfortable. The parents and children huddled together in their loneliness, take too much out of each other. The parents fight; the children rebel. Children need to grow up in larger, more relaxed domestic groups centred on the community rather than on mother's kitchen—something like an Israeli Kibbutz, perhaps, or a Chinese commune.

The recent history of the family does little to substantiate Dr Leach's analysis. Although it is conceivable that society could continue without the family as we know it, efforts to abolish it, or radically alter it, have so far failed. In the U.S.S.R. attempts were made, from 1917 onwards, to undermine the family, for according to Marxist doctrine, stable, monogamous family life is a bulwark of capitalism. Marriage, therefore, in the early days of communism was registered without ceremony, or was valid merely by virtue of a simple declaration of co-habitation; divorce required only an application by one spouse; abortion was by request. At school, children were indoctrinated to put state before family. But the consequences were alarming. Anti-familial policies, it was found, weakened community ties, they were associated with violence and hooliganism among the young, and the birthrate fell dramatically, a threat to both the labour and defence forces. The outcome was that in the thirties the family was reinstated, with many of its bourgeois trappings, as the training ground for socialist children. Solemn marriage ceremonials with the bride in white were allowed, lifelong intent was emphasised, a positive value was put upon motherhood, and children were exhorted to honour their parents, Old Testament fashion. Currently, a handbook for parents, said to be widely read in Russia, places the responsibility for rearing Soviet children appropriately, uncompromisingly in the hands of their parents.

Since the Second World War, a more sophisticated attempt to do without the family as we know it, on Kibbutzim in Israel, is also proving abortive. Here children are reared communally in nurseries staffed by experts, and their parents are relieved of responsibility for them. But as prosperity has grown, parents and children have increasingly assembled as family units for part of the day, and it is said that members of the second generation with fewer economic pressures and less fired by pioneering zeal tend to marry out of the Kibbutz and to live in families as do most other Europeans. As for the Chinese commune we shall have to wait longer before there is adequate evidence to pass judgment.

It would appear from the evidence we have that the family *in some form* is up to now a universal institution and that there is no known society in which it does not comprise a component part of the social structure. It is only in times of revolution and crisis that families will consent to separation, as did husbands, wives and evacuated children during the war. But although families and even whole societies will forgo family life voluntarily for limited periods, up to now the family has re-emerged persistently as an integral part of social structure.

Family forms, however, have great diversity and relatively few of the practices associated with the family can be said to be universal. Nevertheless, it is possible to identify certain patterns of familial behaviour which tend to recur in given circumstances, even although not all families conform to the norms of their own culture: some are oriented towards different value systems, there are great variations in the internal organisation of individual family units, there are differences in family organisation even in the same society between different social strata, and relationships with other societal institutions or structures vary. Furthermore, the family performs different functions in the maintenance of the social structure at different times and in different places. Part of our purpose will be to try to explain why relationships between family organisation and social structure differ, why family forms are so variable and why role requirements and expectations diverge even within our own society.

A complete sociological theory of the family would explain family forms in any culture. In the absence of a general theory of family behaviour, we shall view the family from a variety of perspectives. The first will be externally from that of society. Here we shall be concerned with the family as an institution inter-related with other societal institutions and structures which both limit and stimulate its activities. The family can also be regarded as a relatively autonomous social system, itself made up of a web of interacting elements, so a second perspective will concentrate on its internal structure, its interpersonal relationships, its influence on personality development, on a series of close-ups, in fact. But the family or any other social institution is more than a series of stills; it is always in process and changing. So we shall add a third perspective, the life developmental cycle, which will project the dimension of dynamism on to the small group perspective. Furthermore, a study of the family in complex, urban, industrialised, secularised, specialised and differentiated societies is complicated by the rapidity of social, political and economic change. Whereas many primitive societies while they remained isolated from western influences were relatively static, over many centuries so far as we can tell, in complex societies rapid technological advances have been accompanied by highly dynamic situations in familial structures, as elsewhere in society, which means our concern is with *changing* family life within the context of a wider social structure which is *also changing*. Within this complicated and dynamic wider social structure there are numerous variables such as occupation, class, status, religion and demographic structure, to mention a few, all of which affect particular family structures and which must be taken into account if we are to build an adequate, composite picture of the contemporary family.

Enough has now been said to indicate what we mean by a sociological approach to the study of the family and to show the depth of the cleavage between experts in their interpretation of the data. Like other sociologists, family sociologists aim to develop a body of theory which means, in effect, that in what follows we shall be looking for systematically organised and inter-related propositions about the family which can be validated, or even partially validated, in terms of empirical evidence. Our primary interest and principal goal is to study and explain human behaviour as it relates to the family and marriage in order to achieve a fuller understanding of the processes at work in society. Such an understanding could facilitate the development and implementation of rational and viable social policies.

The emphasis will be on modern Britain, though there will be occasional cross references, particularly to Europe and North America, when they can be used to facilitate understanding.

Part I

Institutional aspects

The family in society

The nature of the family and marriage

For many of us the family constitutes our first experience of social life, and for many also it is the most enduring and permanent social group. It has been maintained by some that the family is essentially a biological unit, centred on the function of reproduction and geared to perpetuating the species. Others have held that its nature is cultural and social, that it *derives* from *society*. Those favouring the biological view argue that the family, regarded as a cohesive group consisting of two parents and their offspring, is not peculiar to man, but is to be found also among a variety of mammals and birds. They maintain that the family is a 'natural' association arising out of the need to care for the young while they are dependent; for human children are produced rather infrequently and in small numbers compared with those of other species and are helpless for a long period, so that continuous care is necessary if enough are to survive to perpetuate the human species. All this may indeed be so, but the human family is peculiar in that it is reinforced by institutions that are indubitably social, and it is the existence of these social institutions, with their embodiment of cultural norms, together with certain cognitive attributes of its members, which principally distinguish the human family from the so-called families of other species.

Although the human family is linked to a whole network of social institutions in society, its closest association is with the supporting institution of marriage which formalises and regularises the relationships between family members. The institution of marriage is essential to the idea of the family as we know it, and the two are indeed often almost indistinguishable and difficult to separate for purposes of analysis, although strictly speaking marriage is an institution within the family. It is only when the meaning of 'family' is stretched to include three or more generations and their collateral relations, that family functions and roles are easily distinguishable from those of marriage. Accordingly, an early consideration of the nature of marriage is imperative, and for this purpose Westermarck's classic definition may be used as a starting point. Marriage, he suggests, is a relation 'of one or more men with one or more women which is recognised by custom or law, and which involves certain rights and duties, both in the case of the parties entering the union and in the case of the children born of it'.[1] Westermarck's definition depicts marriage as unquestionably social and clearly distinguishable from mere biological mating. It highlights the features which constitute the essence of marriage in all societies and in particular that it must be *recognised*, with institutionalised rights and duties attached. Thus casual sexual relationships are excluded. Excluded also are stable relationships which are irregular in the sense of being unrecognised by society, although some of these may in certain circumstances properly be called families if not marriages.

A wide variety of practices are allowed for in Westermarck's definition. It accommodates group marriage. It allows for *polygyny*, that is when one man has more than one wife, an arrangement fairly commonly permitted in societies where prestige attaches to possessions. It covers *polyandry* also, that is when one woman has a plurality of husbands, a situation less usual than polygyny, and associated particularly with isolated mountain or island communities, and with societies in which the male part in reproduction is not understood so that the woman derives power and status from her seemingly magical attributes. It even encompasses a form largely emergent since Westermarck's own day, 'polygamy on the installment plan,' when both men and women have several spouses, but singly, in succession, 'Hollywood' fashion. Westermarck, it will be noted, does not use permanence as a criterion of valid marriage, for divorce has always been permissible in many societies, both primitive and advanced, and is often easy when no bride-price, dowry, or other property settlement is involved. Nevertheless, norms and sanctions for its support frequently underline the importance of marriage as a fairly durable arrangement in most societies. Similarly, Westermarck does not insist that marriage should be voluntary, for marriage by capture is quite legitimate in some societies, and the arranged marriage of convenience or for dynastic reasons is also common.

Children *are* central to Westermarck's conception of marriage, though a marriage can exist where none are born. The position with regard to children is made more explicit by Malinowski, another earlier writer, when he states that marriage is 'the licencing not of sexual intercourse, but of parenthood', which is an important distinction, for again, in many societies, there are legitimate ways of achieving sexual satisfaction outside marriage, ways which are institutionalised. For example, there are societies where a girl is expected to demonstrate her fertility by giving birth to a child before she marries.

Westermarck's definition of marriage can also embrace a wide variety of family forms or structures. It can encompass a *patriarchy*, that is where authority is in the hands of men, and particularly where it is vested in the oldest male member of the family. Less commonly we find a *matriarchy* where power is in the hands of women, as among the Iroquois Indians, for example, whose women had political power, conducted ceremonials and had considerable property rights. Residence may be *patrilocal*, that is the wife goes to the husband when they set up their joint home; or less usually, it may be *matrilocal*, that is when the man joins the bride's family on marriage. A family may be *patrilineal* and *patronymic*; that is when descent is traced through the male, and the family name is taken from the male side; or in some societies we find a *matrilineal-matronymic* arrangement. To give one example, the classical Chinese family, where filial piety was the dominant value and the position of women was debased to that of vehicles for the provision of sons, was patriarchal, patrilineal and patrilocal. However, numerous combinations of these forms can be viable.

It is clear, then, that our own conception of the nature of marriage and of family organisation is only one of a variety of possibilities. The ideal-type marriage in modern Britain is defined in the Report of the Royal Commission on Marriage and Divorce, 1955, as 'a voluntary union for life of one man and one woman to the exclusion of all others'; that is, it is regarded as voluntary, permanent, and as strictly monogamous. It is this ideal which the law attempts to implement. The ideal and the actual rarely coincide, and as a recognition of the realities in a secularised society, the law, from time to time, makes concessions which modify the full impact of what is in fact part of the Christian ethic on marriage.

This definition of marriage does not specify the procreation of children as an essential element in marriage. It does not exclude the secular view that puts the personal happiness of the spouses as the chief end in marriage, and the procreation of children as a matter of personal choice, rather than an obligation as it is in the view of those who give priority to the welfare of society. Nevertheless, children remain central to our conception of marriage. The obligation to have children features in the marriage service of the established church, and in other forms of marriage ceremonies also. Marriage in any meaningful sense involves rights and obligations, and of these the ones which carry the most insistent societal sanctions are those relating to the children of a marriage. It is the protection of the interests of children which forms the principal argument for permanent, monogamous unions. Most contemporary writers on marriage also appear to regard children, or the intention to have children, as a near-essential ingredient of a full marriage relationship. Gorer,[2] for example, defines marriage as 'living together, making a home together, making a life together, and raising children'. He and others have suggested that the desire for love and sexual satisfaction, the principal components of childless unions, are in reality secondary in importance to the fact of marriage itself, the common life and the presence of children.

The expectation that a full marriage relationship will include caring for the children born of the union does not preclude emphasis on the importance of love and sexual fulfilment. Some confusion tends to arise because love in our society is sometimes equated with an impossible romanticism, highly commercialised in entertainment and advertising. Many would also distinguish between love and sexual gratification. Although both may be present in a good marriage relationship, much writing about 'love' confuses it with 'sex'. Love, according to Alex Comfort,[3] includes not only physical attraction and satisfaction, but also 'mutual respect, mutual communication and a strong desire to protect one another without any corresponding wish to manipulate or mould'. With this kind of love, he maintains, there is little temptation to deviate from the norms of permanence and monogamy. Thus many would insist that marriage in our society is ideally 'voluntary, monogamous, permanent, for the raising of children and for sexual gratification'.

Functions of the family

A proper consideration of the whole familial context would require an interdisciplinary approach to give due weight to habitat and to genetic, physiological and psychological factors. The classic sociological approach to the study of the family is to treat it as an institution interacting with other social institutions and forming part of a larger social structure. Social institutions, in the sense of established patterns of behaviour, are seen as interdependent. In the process of interaction, family behaviour responds to external situations and is modified by them, and similarly, the other institutions with which it interacts are modified also.

In simple societies all aspects of life are related to the family or kinship structure, and the family is the most important unit of social organisation. Indeed family and society are synonymous. The family, used in this wide sense to mean the whole kingroup, comprises the total social structure in such societies, and in them it dominates all other institutions, and is the key to understanding them. In more complex societies it has less influence, and indeed the greater the complexity of the society, the greater the variety of external agencies with which the family interacts. As complexity increases in the form of industrialisation and urbanisation, the family will interact increasingly with the economy, the polity, the judiciary, the military, with the educational system, with the welfare and social security agencies, in fact with every aspect of community life, and as it is constrained to develop closer relations with other major institutions in society, the family unit tends to be reduced in size. The family which is fully functional as a social institution tends to be extended vertically to include three or more generations and horizontally to include collateral relations. The contemporary family, denuded of many of its institutional functions, is typically the *nuclear* or *conjugal* or *elementary* family (the terms are used interchangeably) consisting of a married couple and their offspring only.

Many cross-cultural studies have been made in the attempt to identify the factors which have some degree of universality. All families, at whatever level of development and of whatever model, perform certain functions for society and for the individual, and all these functions are inter-related. It can, indeed, be argued that the continued existence and influence of the family as a social institution is accounted for in terms of the functions it performs on behalf of society and which contribute to the maintenance of society. From this standpoint, family patterns of behaviour are related to the norms of the society of which the family forms part and, furthermore, they tend to uphold the normative patterns of that society. There is a mutual interacting and supportive relationship in this respect between the family and society, and it can be observed that in periods when societal norms are being disrupted or are changing rapidly, the family, being an important element in the total social structure, changes also. The study of the family as an institution is thus slanted towards analysing the existing and changing relationships between the family and society, rather than towards analysing the nuclear family as a social system in its own right, which is the approach of many contemporary family sociologists.

Certain functions, now carried out by the family, must be performed by some agency or agencies for any society to survive. The power of the family as a societal institution can be measured by the effectiveness with which it carries out functions which are essential for the maintenance of a society in the sense that the society would collapse if they were not performed. Of first priority is the continuity of society and this requires the replacement of population. Reproduction, carried on legitimately in accordance with rules which are understood and have a general acceptability, is usually regarded as the central institutional function of the family. By regulating reproduction, the family not only ensures the continuity of the species but that of the culture also, for procreation alone does not serve to maintain the continuity of society. It is the family which undertakes the socialisation of the child during his long period of dependency, and the more complex the society, the longer is the period of dependency. But at every level of development from the simple to the complex, children must be nurtured and reared in ways that will ensure their survival in numbers sufficient for population replacement, and they must also be prepared for life in the society in which they will live. Appropriate skills and knowledge are passed on by means of training and instruction, initially in a family setting. In a simple society, the family will remain wholly responsible; as complexity of social organisation increases, so does the number of external agencies involved in education and training.

In the family setting too, the child first learns to handle some of the different types of personal relationships that he will find later in the wider society. The parent–child and the sibling–sibling relationships give him experience of both authoritative and egalitarian type relationships, and an opportunity to come to terms with them. He also learns something of the dynamics of group life, of how to live together with others, and share. He learns to defer to the interests and wishes of the group and to forgo at times his personal preferences. Indeed, in simple societies the needs and interests of the group as a whole usually take precedence over those of individuals, and life at this level can be harsh, as in nomadic tribes, where, for example, the parturient woman may be left to catch up with the group if and when she can. There is room for sentiment and finer feeling only in more developed societies.

The family, as an agent of social control, teaches the child the limits of tolerated behaviour. It introduces him to the acceptable ideas of right and wrong. He absorbs the moral standards of his family, their attitudes to honesty, cupidity, violence, and so on. However, the family, in exercising its function of social control, is itself influenced by the wider society. For example, where community sanctions break down, family authority is enfeebled also, as can be observed in times of disaster. The process is also well documented for immigrant groups; the traditional sanctions of peasant communities manifested in patriarchal authority and religious observance lose their hold on second-generation settlers. Similarly the family moulds the child's taste. Much is not consciously taught but is absorbed by the child from his family environment; his own taste later is likely to reflect what he has seen at home, whether it be flights of pottery geese on the wall, watercolours by an aunt, or more modern art forms such as bits of old kitchen ware glued together.

The influence of the family is directed not only to the maintenance of its own standards but also towards the maintenance of those of the society in which it is located. It has at its command all the sanctions, direct and indirect, of a primary group, and by means of them it impels the individual not only to identify with the family group and so uphold its standards, but it also exerts pressures on its members to conform to the norms, laws, mores and folkways of the wider community of which it forms a part and in this way contributes to the maintenance of societal standards also.

Attitudes of particular families may, of course, differ from those of the society at large. The mores of a delinquent sub-culture may be transmitted. If, for example, the values of honesty and self-control are not accepted in the family group, then deviations from the societal norms may become manifest in drunkenness, overspending, shoplifting, and the like. This is not to say that every family conforming to societal norms follows the same pattern of behaviour, but only that the majority of families express their individuality, outwardly at least, in non-deviant ways. Each may have its own patterns of entertaining and leisure pursuits, its own eccentricities of dress, food and interior decoration, its in-jokes and private rituals. These minor deviations contribute to the cohesion of particular family units. Similarly, conformity to the general norms of society, in intent if not always in fact, and the expression of conformity through participation in community ceremonies also give the family importance as an agent of societal cohesion. Indeed, by its participation in the more general social activities it provides a sense of legitimacy for the group life of the society.

The family as a link between the individual and society

The family is also for most people the most essential link between the individual and society in so far as it provides the individual with an identity in the wider society. The family is an involuntary group and the status derived from an involuntary group is always ascribed. From the family the individual initially receives a socially *ascribed status*, so that membership of a family gives the child a position in the social hierarchy. The absence of an ascribed family status is illegitimacy. Legitimacy, through membership of a family group constituted according to the rules of the society, confers on the child a position that defines his relationship to other members of the society, which means that he has certain ascribed positions which the illegitimate child does not. Some statuses are inherited, for example a name or an office, and it is through the family that descent is traced and the title to them legitimated.

The ascriptive importance of the family varies at different stages of social development and also from society to society. In a rigidly stratified society such as one with a caste system or a closed class system which effectively blocks social mobility, the child is likely to remain in his family-ascribed position throughout his life. Modern Britain has a fairly open social hierarchy and ascribed status need not be permanent where there can be movement up and down the social scale. Since the industrial revolution, with its concomitant of intensified urban living, and particularly during the present century with its extended educational opportunities, there have been more chances of achieved status for more people. The anonymity of town life has made it possible to conceal or forget family origins, and to assume an identity independently of the family, whereas in a small community the history and reputation of his family are common knowledge when the young adult emerges to take his place. Indeed, in the urban–industrial situation he may gain materially if he drops his family connections, though he may in the process lose important sources of emotional well-being and adjustment, and also his sense of individuality, his identity as a person as distinct from his identity as a mere position in the social hierarchy.

Changes such as these mean that the family no longer provides security of status in the outside world as it does in more closed societies. At almost all social levels the family member is now faced by the necessity to achieve his own status. The child must make his mark in school and in his play groups, the adult male is faced with job competitiveness, and the adult female is in a similarly competitive position for, as the recipient of her husband's status, she must marry as 'well' as possible if she is to retain or improve her own status. Thus, in an open society such as our own, achieved statuses have gained in importance, and the importance of the ascribed statuses derived from the family have been correspondingly reduced. Nevertheless, although the status-conferring function of the family has been greatly eroded, modern Britain remains a socially stratified society, and each family has a class-status position which is an important determinant of the class-status positions of its members. The child's familial ascriptive position is a starting point and as such important, even although his initial position can be modified later. His *achieved status* is the position he makes for himself, with or without the help of his family. Family background has been shown to have considerable influence on achieved status,[4] for on it depends the number and height of the hurdles to be cleared by the socially upwardly mobile. When the child comes to take part in extra-familial group activities, those open to him are determined largely by his family's position in the status hierarchy and this situation persists throughout childhood.

There is a positive correlation, with some reservations such as the non-acceptance of the *nouveaux-riches*, between property, money and status. Property is transmitted by inheritance, and descent and eligibility are conferred through the family. The father's occupation and income are of particular significance in an achievement-oriented society. In so far as family status is indicated by the consumption of clothes, cars, boats, or whatever the current fads demand, the father's job-success is the most obvious link. Domestic arrangements, which interlock with consumption patterns, are also sensitive barometers of status; for example, furnishings and bric-à-brac; the food chosen, the way it is served and eaten, and at what time of day; the frequency of bathing and the rituals centred on the bathroom, to mention only a few. The whole family takes on the father's status, which is thus basically outside the control of the other members, although they, too, can enhance it, for example by achievement in school or sport, or in the case of the wife, by being attractive and witty, entertaining judiciously and making the 'right' friends among other wives, or by having a personal fortune. Similarly education is status-giving and the type and degree of the father's occupational attainment are associated with his educational level. Race may be another important indicator of status. So may religious denomination; upwardly mobile families not infrequently change their denomination somewhere along the continuum stretching from the evangelical to the episcopalian. Other organisations to which the parents belong also have significance, so has the degree to which they participate in community affairs, the ways in which they use their leisure, how they spend or save their money, and the neighbourhood in which they live. Length of residence in a neighbourhood also adds to family status. This start in life limits the kinds of people the child will meet, the sorts of experiences that will come his way, and which will shape his behaviour, tastes, attitudes and speech. The occupational choices open to him are similarly effectively defined by family origin and the experiences it opens up. All of these statuses, ascribed and achieved, add up to a composite position in society by which he can be pigeonholed and by which he identifies himself.

The life chances of the individual are thus intimately affected by his initial family background and there are usually distinct limits to the extent to which he may change his statuses. Furthermore, although occupation can alter status irrespective of family, those who succeed in effecting a radical change are often only partially accepted in the status groups to which they seek entry.

For the individual the family meets other needs which are both biologically derived and also culturally prescribed, and in meeting these needs for individuals it again plays a part in maintaining the total social structure. It provides a legitimate outlet for the sexual urge. Stable and recognised sex relationships have psychological importance. Women need freedom from mental and material anxieties when they are engaged in producing and rearing children, and from this freedom follows the practical and societally important consequence of enhancing the chances of survival of a new life; for abortion and infanticide are commoner when the parental mating is an unacceptable one in the society. Stability in sex relationships also lessens the likelihood that men will dissipate their energies in sexual competition, and so indirectly increases their capacity to focus their effort towards the welfare of the family group in economically productive ways and in providing protection.

For both sexes emotional security and warmth are important. Some achieve them in part through parenthood which is a source of fulfilment for many despite the hardships and frustrations which may also attach to it. Parenthood, as a means of emotional gratification, is most rewarding in this respect when the culture values children highly as, for example, when they perform an economic role, or are required as heirs to property, or, as in our own culture, are not only social assets, but increasingly status symbols also.

To sum up, the family performs important functions for society and for the individual in society. It provides population replacements, and it acts as an agent of socialisation, social control, and social cohesion. It identifies, and supplies identities for, individuals within the social hierarchy. It is not an end in itself, but it exists to solve the problems involved in meeting certain universal human needs, both societal and individual, and it is an intensely active agency in doing so. The *detail* of its activity in this respect varies from society to society.

Industrialisation, urbanisation and secularisation

Industrialisation

Because the family appears as a component of social structure in every known society, does not mean that it has equal significance in maintaining social structures at different times and in different places.

The usual descriptions of the pre-industrial family are frequently stereotyped and somewhat romanticised idealisations founded on a belief in what family life was like in a remote, idyllic, non-existent past, so it must be remembered that the 'classic model' of the pre-industrial family is only an approximation to any actual situation. Further, in so far as it is a real approximation it can be valid only for fairly remote geographical situations. Many families have always lived in towns and only some of those would resemble the pre-industrial 'model'. Nevertheless in the past a much larger proportion of the population lived from the land, so it is not without usefulness to make a few cautious generalisations, provided we remain aware of their limitations.

It seems beyond reasonable doubt, and there is much circumstantial evidence of their reality in the literature of Western Europe, that there were in the past, when agriculture was the predominant source of livelihood, many large households consisting not only of the nuclear family of husband, wife and their children, but comprising a line of descendants, perhaps three or four generations, a selection of collateral blood relations of all ages and both sexes, together with relatives by adoption, and perhaps in some cases servants who were regarded as 'family', although the latter fall outside the scope of the usual definitions of family membership. Apart from the biological functions which are common to all types of familial structures, such families provided a total way of life catering for all the dimensions of work and play within a closely united kingroup. They lived closely, co-operatively and were organised for mutual supportiveness. They performed important economic functions, and on the classic model they were economically self-supporting, supplying all their own needs for food, clothing and shelter by their own efforts. Husband and wife in such a structure were of great importance to one another, for in a productive unit they perform a complicated web of inter-related roles, a situation which makes for stable and durable marriage. All other needs, too, were met within the confines of the family. Individual security was ensured, for the family cared for the young and the old, the sick and the physically and mentally handicapped. Life itself was protected when violence arose, and the family property was conserved and if possible enlarged. Socialisation and education to enable members of the new generation to acquire the skills, mores and norms appropriate to their way of life, took place largely within the family. Religious observance also was a family affair. Similarly justice was dispensed internally, on behalf of the group, which had invested this and other authority by tradition in the patriarch. All in all, his position was one of considerable power in the prototype situation, which calls for not only a figurehead and representative, but for someone with strength and authority great enough to organise production and allocate work, and who will take final responsibility for making decisions which will affect the prosperity, welfare and harmony of the whole family. It follows, too, that fully functional families of the pre-industrial type had a great degree of control over their members, for the members were, because of the nature of the structure, more dependent on the family for material and emotional satisfactions than is the case today.

The family responds to changes in other parts of the social structure and many sources or agents of change are to be found outside rather than within the family. Dramatic modifications of family structure were precipitated by the impact of industrialisation, and the remotely situated wholly self-sufficient type of family became virtually extinct in our own country when the domestic system of the early industrial revolution gave way to the factory system, and production in the economic sense moved out of the home. For many, workplace and home were now separated with a degree of clarity which had rarely been the case in a simpler form of economic organisation. The nearest survival of the traditional pre-industrial family model in the modern world is in peasant economies in areas which are not yet highly industrialised, and vestiges can also be found in rural families in the British Isles (see Ch. 3).

Among the important consequences of the replacement of domestic industries by the factory system was the creation of a new social group, whose members congregated in the towns to sell their sole marketable asset, labour, and thus the economic security of the family became more tenuous than had formerly been the case. The separation of home and work also had profound effects on day-to-day family life. It broke up the close and frequent interaction of husbands and wives, parents and children. As the process of industrialisation has intensified, and as systems of public transport have developed, it has become feasible to travel long distances to work, or to school, and the daily dispersal of the family to office, factory, shop and school has now become institutionalised. At first, when the distances involved were small, the family was often reunited for all its meals, including the one at midday. Now, as fathers commute ever greater distances to work, they may be absent during all or most of the waking hours of their children. The long daily absence of the principal breadwinner has had its effect on the internal authority structure of the family, too. The mother, particularly if she is at home rather than out at work, is frequently left to take entire responsibility for all the day-to-day decisions with regard to the management of the household and the children. As the principal spender and arbiter of taste, her status and authority have been enhanced, even when she works solely in the domestic sphere, and as a corollary, that of the father eroded.[1]

Industrialisation has also altered the balance of power in the family in so far as it has created new types of jobs, jobs which could be done by women. So, for women, jobs became a possible alternative to marriage, an alternative to subservience to husbands or fathers. A woman no longer needed to remain 'the ceremonial consumer' of what her husband produced. This, too, has made for greater equality between the sexes and for a decline in male authority. Technology and the science that begets it have played a part, too, not only in creating jobs for women, but also in enabling women to take them up, by reducing the drudgery of household chores, and lessening the risk of unwanted pregnancies. Some products of technology immediately spring to mind in these connections, among them contraceptives, running water, electricity and labour-saving devices of all kinds. Another impact of technology on family life has been the provision of the means to improved standards of homemaking and of comfort in the home. The scientific advances in medicine have also had a liberating effect by helping to improve the health of the family.

Industrialisation and the separation of home and work have been accompanied by a reduction in the size of households. Grandparents, aunts and other relatives lost their traditional activities within the family, such as making clothes, preserving fruit and vegetables, nursing the sick, supervising the children and so on, all of which had in the past contributed to the maintenance and to the cohesion of family life, for with industrialisation and the increasing availability of commercial supplies, this mêlée of kin became simply so many extra mouths to be fed out of the possibly inadequate wages of the frequently lone breadwinner. Ousted from their useful roles as family members they were ill-equipped to adapt to the demands of an industrialised society, and the rigours of old age or spinsterhood had to be faced without the security of a family status.

In a situation in which there is frequently no place for the individual within the family, he is largely emancipated from any prolonged dependence upon it. He sets his own standard of living after an initial start given him by his family of origin, and is thus freed from many of the obligations which might accrue had he remained one of its active members. His pressing responsibilities are limited to the clearly defined boundaries of his family of procreation. Sometimes exceptions are made of ageing parents, but others such as brothers, sisters and their progeny, are usually excluded, except marginally, from the obligations of mutual supportiveness.

Accordingly, in times of adversity such as sickness, accident, unemployment or natural disaster, the individual is extremely vulnerable for he has few institutionalised claims on his kinsmen and he may undergo great hardship, and become dependent on the state or a charity for succour. Unless he has accumulated resources of his own, his relative freedom from family obligations is enjoyed at the expense of his security, in a world in which he may easily become the victim of circumstances perhaps because his skills have become obsolete, or his work has been in a dying industry, or he has been caught up in world events such as a trade recession, or trading patterns have changed due to political uncertainties abroad. In all such contingencies, adjustment of the individual to changed circumstances tends to be more disquieting than in an integrated family structure.

As industrialisation gained momentum erratic, piecemeal, uncoordinated charity became insufficient to alleviate the new privations, and many self-respecting unfortunates were constrained to resort to a harsh Poor Law which carried with it loss of independence and the stigma of pauperism. This situation was to some extent resolved by extra-familial agencies, first charitable and later statutory, which gradually took over the protective functions of the family, functions for which it had once assumed the whole responsibility; and indeed the increasing complexity of the culture now demands specialised agencies for their efficient organisation. Thus today we look to the police to protect life and property. To protect the individual against social hazards, there are a variety of services provided by voluntary organisations, in addition to the whole apparatus of the welfare state, with its provision for all contingencies 'from the cradle to the grave', as Beveridge put it. The insurance scheme feather-beds unemployment, accident, death, disaster and other misfortunes. The health service, with its hospitals, homes and various community organisations, cares for the sick, the handicapped, the old and the insane. There are general welfare services, concerned with the needs of children deprived of home life, and to help others with defective home conditions there are housing subsidies. There are measures for easing the transition from school to employment, there is provision for leisure pursuits in the form of youth clubs, drama, participant sport and the like, geared particularly to the needs of young people whose families no longer supervise this facet of their lives. For some, both young and old, commercial agencies rather than the family often provide leisure

3

activities in the form of coffee bars, gambling clubs, dance halls, spectator sport, pools, television, theatres and sometimes, too, 'improving' activities. Legislative provision for holidays with pay has made an annual holiday away from the family a possibility for many, and the day trip to the sea is giving way increasingly to a couple of weeks on the Majorcan beaches. Furthermore, judicial and religious activities, once the prerogatives of the head of the family, have been ceded to the state or other corporate bodies. Education, from nursery school level to graduate study and for all from the severely retarded to the genius I.Q., has become the province of the state or of some other specialised organisation. Indeed even home-making itself, surely central to any conception of family living, today includes organising and co-ordinating the use of publicly or commercially available services and products, the contemporary alternative to their provision within the home.

All this can be summed up by concluding that there has been a decline in the institutional functions of the family, a decline which is closely associated with changes external to the family in the economic structure of society, changes which have been accompanied by far-reaching social changes also.

Urbanisation

Changes in the institutional aspects of the family have been associated not only with industrialisation and the growth in scientific knowledge and technology, but also with urbanism, which has intensified as industrialism has grown. Men have lived in cities for thousands of years, so it is not accurate to speak of urbanism as though it were a product of the industrial revolution alone. But certain aspects of urban life certainly are, and these too have had an effect on the family, although it is difficult to disentangle the urbanisation and industrialisation threads which are closely intertwined. The types of social organisation and social behaviour that emerge from urbanism are often explained in terms of the variables size, density, heterogeneity and anonymity. There will be differences in the manifestations of urbanism as these variables combine in differing proportions, and the characteristics associated with urban living will be at their most accentuated in the large city and the megalopolis.

All this adds up to a new way of life with effects on family functions and roles. Sheer density of population has necessitated the assumption of public responsibility for services which impinge on family life, and in particular for public health, clean water supplies and sewage disposal. These are benefits to the family. Density makes feasible the public supply of gas and electricity so raising standards of comfort, and also systems of public transport, which not only give families a greater choice of locality in which to live, but enable jobs to be changed more readily when they need not be located in close proximity to home. Nevertheless, density makes for cramped and expensive living conditions. To achieve reasonable privacy and freedom from criticism or interference, certain barriers must be erected and defensive attitudes emerge such as 'keeping oneself to oneself'. In these conditions there tend to be few primary group relationships outside the nuclear family, less opportunity to become closely involved with a neighbourhood or extended kinship group. The sense of 'belonging,' born of living together for generations, is absent or weak. It is only in exceptional circumstances that a wider group spirit becomes evident, for example neighbourhood collections after an accident, or the camaraderie of street parties to celebrate an event such as the Coronation; and even so cohesiveness of this kind tends to be ephemeral and limited to the occasion.

Towns are characterised, too, by the diversity of the inhabitants, people diverse in occupation, race, cultural background, religious and other beliefs. In such circumstances misunderstandings easily arise, which is another reason for the wariness exercised by urbanites in making social contacts and for keeping them at an impersonal, superficial level. Secondary group relationships assume importance; the urban dweller joins clubs and special interest groups, which may be dispersed in localities distant from his home neighbourhood, and which bring with them disparate and segmented personal relationships. The urbanite may well acquire a large acquaintance in this way, but few or no friends about whom he knows much. The individual counts for little in a heterogeneous society of secondary group relationships. Primary groups are weak, and in times of trouble he has, or may have, the nuclear family to fall back on. But his links with the family are tenuous when it has ceased to be an economic unit, and are often dependent merely on personal whim or fortuitous events. So for some urbanites the family, as the principal remaining primary group in the lives of individuals, ceases to be a reliable buffer or permanent shelter in adversity. Density of population makes the possibility of help from neighbours feasible if they hear of the trouble, but they have no recognised obligation. Many people do indeed find the anxieties and isolation too much, a fact which is reflected in rates of mental illness, suicide, crime and other social deviations, which are higher in urban than they are in rural areas in which family and community life are still more integrated than in the towns.

Although the 'anomic' conditions may precipitate social and personal disorganisation for some, for others life in towns, lived on the principle of secondary contacts which emancipate them from the social and emotional controls of intimate family and kinship groups, has opened up opportunities for personal advancement and social mobility. Families that are highly integrated into a kinship network or into a community inhibit the social mobility of their members. They hinder geographical mobility (a necessity for the smooth functioning of the economy), for whole kingroups are too cumbersome to respond sensitively to the changing demands of the economy; and they hinder contact with other social classes because of the social demands of the kingroup itself, both of which are types of behaviour which facilitate upward social mobility. Conversely, for the individual or the nuclear family unit who seize chances of upward social mobility, perhaps by moving to a new district, the importance of the wider kingroup is reduced and consequently the emotional links become attenuated.

The urban family thus tends to be a mobile one, physically and socially, and for both reasons it tends toward a certain rootlessness. For a family which may move on every two years, and many do, belongings are limited; there can be no hoarding of potentially useful junk in attics. People are as acquisitive as ever, perhaps more so, but possessions are more ephemeral. Ably abetted by the depth advertisers, families buy goods to give immediate pleasure and discard them with little regret to facilitate the next move. The same goes for friends. Ties with other families are brittle and can be broken without disrupting lives irrevocably; friendships are cast aside, like threadbare furnishings, at each move. Without time to strengthen its roots, the mobile family depends on transient associations at each stop, virtually leading the life of the transit camp with just a few embellishments and refinements. At the same time individuals depend entirely on the other members of the small nuclear family for the really close emotional ties which have such importance for personal stability.

Secularisation

Also intimately associated with industrialisation and with urbanisation is secularisation. The growth of knowledge in other fields, and particularly in the sciences, has undermined traditional religious authority, and presented a challenge to attitudes that formerly had religious sanction. Darwin's work cast doubt on the biblical account of the origin of the world and of man. The application of scientific knowledge to the ailments of the body and the mind led not only to the replacement of herbs by antibiotics, but also to a questioning of traditional codes of conduct in relation to sex, chastity, marriage and fidelity, all of which have been central to family life in communities subscribing, even if only nominally, to the Christian ethic.

Many of our own societal norms and values concerning the family derive from Christianity, which itself owes much to the Judaic tradition which preceded it. The Israelites exalted and in a sense consecrated the family through their imagery of God as Father, albeit an awe-inspiring Father whose sometimes harsh treatment of his children was to be accepted without question. All this was in the nomadic and patriarchal tradition, which demanded that the individual should be subordinate to the group, as was the polygyny which operated to secure the necessary strong male line of succession. Christianity retained the family as a central idea, but the Christian family became one in which the individual had a place in his own right. The limitation of sexual activity within marriage, which means chastity before and fidelity after marriage, and the ideal of a lifelong and monogamous union spring, at least in part, from a belief in the worth of the individual. So does the emphasis on the sanctity of human life embodied in the prohibition of abortion and, in some denominations, of contraception. Christian teaching has opposed practices such as prostitution regarded as undermining the dignity of the individual and as threatening family life within which the individual ideally finds his fulfilment. Emphasis on the marriage vows as sacred also stems from the belief that a stable family environment is the best for the child and divorce laws up to now have been designed to make the break-up of a marriage difficult. It has indeed been suggested that the Christian striving for standards which include love, kindness, tolerance and forgiveness, promotes attitudes conducive to stable and happy marriages. Thus it can be seen that attitudes derived from the Christian ethic permeate our norms of family life, and many of them are accepted even among those whose outlook is wholly secular.

There may of course be a tendency to regard all past generations as devout, which could be misleading. Research in the Cumberland village of Gosforth, for example, brought to light much evidence culled from nineteenth-century parish magazines of real irreverence and a positive indifference to religion, surprising in a rural community where traditional and conservative attitudes tend to linger long. Nevertheless, there can be little doubt of the increasing secularisation of society and of its effects on family life. Open affirmations of faith are on the decline. Family prayers were routine in Victorian middle-class families, as was the saying of grace before and after meals, and regular attendance at a place of worship by the whole family. Although it must be remembered that the middle classes are prone to conventional observances, a common faith, openly and frequently reaffirmed together, tends to promote feelings of well-being, stability and sentiments of solidarity within the family group, and organised religion is ceasing to perform this cohesive function for the family. Church attendance, an outward sign and the measure usually used, continues to decline among many sections of the population and is a cause of concern to most denominations.

Although there is a decreasing interest in the formal aspects of religion, some ceremonies and rites, particularly those of baptism, marriage, confirmation and those surrounding death, still attract appreciable numbers and there are often large congregations at Christmas, Easter and the Harvest Festivals, despite indifference for the rest of the year. All of them can be said to have social as well as spiritual significance. Whatever the motivations for these attendances, even when they are wholly social or secular, they mean more family participation and serve to cement the feeling of solidarity as all institutionalised rituals appear to do. Participation in the rituals surrounding religious observance endows them with particular meanings for family members, and so helps to define and set limits to family goals, and, furthermore, to form bonds with other like-minded families. The same applies to participation in the fringe activities of the churches, such as outings.

Families can and do develop their own rituals such as birthday gatherings, picnics and outings to particular places which may become a form of pilgrimage with quasi-religious integrative effects for the family. The new secular religions such as science and medicine have their adherents also, and are surrounded by dogma and ritual no less than the longer established religions. But there are few who would regard a blind faith in the infallibility of science, and a regular observance of the ritual of visiting the doctor or of prostration on the analyst's couch, as being as functional in the promotion of family pride and group identity as were the older conventions which emphasised, as the new quasi-religions do not, the importance of family life by insisting on the honourable estate of parenthood, and on the sanctity of marriage.

There are many examples which could be quoted to illustrate the current uncertainties in relation to marriage and sexual behaviour in a society lukewarm to the traditional authority of the churches. A decade ago an article in a magazine addressed specifically to those contemplating marriage, and published by no less a body than the British Medical Association, questioned the wisdom of the conventional expectation of pre-nuptial chastity:

Surely the individual should have the right to choose between being chaste or unchaste, always assuming that this was not detrimental to the society of which he was a part.[2]

Public uproar followed the publication of this article. More recently, the declaration of a university teacher of his view that men and women students should be permitted to share bedrooms if they wished to do so was followed by vigorous protestations by an outraged public and by threats from a local authority to withhold financial aid from the university concerned. Such incidents clearly demonstrate the prevalent vacillations which surround the 'permissive' sexual morality and the general uneasiness of the public on the subject of marriage at a time when the relationship of the family to society is changing and in its transition appears ambiguous.

Kinship and neighbourhood

The term *nuclear* family is used to mean the group consisting of husband, wife, and their children. So much is clear. But 'the family' is also used to denote vertical relationships between the generations, an extensive range of collateral relationships, and also some affinities which include those by marriage, not by blood. Unfortunately the terms used to describe these other relationships are not used consistently in the literature. For simplicity, and at the risk of oversimplification, we shall here use the term *extended family* to denote close blood relations and their spouses who are outside the immediate nuclear family; and *kingroup* or *kinship network* as inclusive terms to denote all known and recognised relationships of every degree of affinity. Kinship in our society carries with it no obligations which are enforceable, except in respect of certain very close relations.

The isolation of the nuclear family, segregated from kin within its separate dwelling, bereft of social contacts and of help in times of trouble, was much emphasised in the textbooks of two or three decades ago. Anthropological studies of complex, western societies in recent years suggest, however, that this isolation, supposedly an inevitable accompaniment of industrialisation and urbanisation, both of which it was assumed were antipathetic to the large family group, has been somewhat exaggerated. Some of these studies have revealed that kinship is still a structural reality and still has functional significance in modern industrial societies and that relationships at varying degrees of distance have a place in the functioning of the nuclear family, although their role has not yet been sufficiently clarified.

For many, kinship provides a ready-made source of companionship. This assumes great importance when physical mobility is restricted and at social levels where money is really short, but it is also a feature of life at levels where cars, travel and golf club membership can be afforded. A correspondence in the composition of households within a kingroup, for example children of complementary ages and sexes, and in the stage reached in the family cycle of development, have been shown to reinforce the kin structure. Similarities in other respects, too, such as income, occupation and leisure-time pursuits make for common interests and so for kinship solidarity.

Kinship carries with it a certain degree of acceptance; kinsmen are not usually turned away. There is abundant evidence to show that the young man who appears on the doorstep, be it in the metropolis or in a Welsh valley, and announces himself as 'Ethel's boy from Halifax', or the appropriate equivalent, can expect to be offered a meal and a bed, and may well be received with great warmth.[1] Even if kinsmen are sometimes hypercritical, demanding, stupid, boring, unattractive and generally uncongenial, they are often also interested and accepting.

However, kin have been shown to be selective in seeking out those with whom they wish to be friendly. Kinship selectivity is affected by social status, and the degree of interaction by the direction of social mobility. The upwardly mobile have been found to avoid over-familiarity with their kin and the downwardly mobile are sometimes cold-shouldered by their kin, practices disruptive of kinship solidarity. Kinship is also commonly used as a vehicle of social mobility at various social levels. This has been documented among contemporary residents in a nineteenth-century tenement block, and it is not un-known for the socially aspiring middle class to dash seventy miles across a county merely to drink a few cocktails with a higher-status kinsman who already has an entrée to the desired social milieu. But although there is a preference for consorting with kinsmen of higher social standing, those who have risen on the socio-economic scale do not necessarily drop their humbler kin entirely. It has been shown in a number of studies that women in particular entertain their poorer kinswomen because in many cases of the strength of common interests in children and domestic matters, although they do not necessarily invite them to meet their new and grander acquaintance.

Interest in and exchange of family news is a feminine preoccupation, as women generally have a wider range of knowledge of the minutiae of kinship connectedness than do men. The optimum position for the most extensive kinship knowledge is early middle age. In his study of families living in an old London tenement Firth found that women in early middle age would be aware of inter-relationships over five generations, or exceptionally seven, and that it was not uncommon to be able to count two hundred kin, although not all might be known by name, and effective, purposeful social interaction took place with a smaller number. Among long-established members of the middle class there is often kin knowledge in greater depth. Many seem to claim descent, and indeed are able to produce relics, passed down in the family, from personages who had some claim to fame in their own generation such as a minor poet or explorer of the eighteenth or nineteenth century. Newer members of the middle class also show an interest in their forebears, and to meet the desire for ancestors a flourishing genealogical industry has grown up. Kinship knowledge increases with social level and those with the greatest degree of kinship knowledge both in depth and collaterally are, presumably, those whose names appear in *Burke's Peerage*. But in all social strata an important factor contributing to the solidarity of the kingroup is the existence of someone at the centre of a communication network, who receives and disseminates information by every means available. The actual *modus operandi* will vary by social stratum and with the degree of geographical dispersion; the 'Mum' of Bethnal Green will not write letters or give parties in the manner of her more literate or affluent counterpart. But the channel of communication is likely to be through women generally, and often through one matriarchal figure in particular, who provides a highly personalised computer-type service, sifting, sorting, arranging, realigning and distributing family news.

The closeness of the mother–daughter relationship has been identified as a crucial variable in the understanding of patterns of sociality among kinsmen in several social strata. The most widely quoted source, although it was not the first study of this kind, is a study of family and kinship in the 'traditional' working-class district of

Bethnal Green and of the changes which followed the rehousing of many of its younger residents on a new L.C.C. estate twenty miles distant. The investigators discovered that although the old-style working-class marriage relationship and family life is disappearing even in Bethnal Green and being replaced by the new-style marriage of companionship, many characteristics of the traditional pattern persist. Both marriage partners are often born in the same or an adjacent district. Newly-weds set up house in the bride's mother's home, or nearby. if the mother has influence with the rent collector, which further cements the relationship in which the daughter is characteristically very dependent on her mother. Frequently they see one another several times a day, and as a by-product married sisters often meet continually in their mother's house. The mother assumes a matriarchal role, and a pattern of mutual supportiveness and reciprocal services is maintained, the mother helping with confinements, advice, child care (the grandchildren often go to her straight from school for tea), her daughter(s) caring for her in return as she ages. On marriage a daughter thus remains involved with an extended family within which her mother is a powerful matriarchal figure who keeps the group together as a highly functional unit in which she herself has an accepted place until extreme old age.

Domestic affairs in this type of family are petticoat dominated. But the fact of kinship regulates the lives of both sexes in the traditional working-class area. Because houses are small, overcrowded, lacking in facilities and with the paraphernalia of child care such as damp washing much in evidence, the men, partly from necessity, tend to find their social life in an exclusively male group in pubs and clubs, so that consequently men's and women's lives, at work and leisure, are separate. A man's associates will be his workmates and his male kin; and there will be some correspondence between the two, for in this kind of area many men still follow their fathers' occupations, and it is still common for jobs to be obtained by relatives 'speaking for' one another. Whole families of men, including in-laws, often give their allegiance to one firm, and see one another in their spare time as well, so forming close relationships just as female kin do. But the two sexes lead largely separate lives in two groups, one dominated by female interests, the other by male. And in family matters, apart from the final one of controlling the purse strings, the women are supreme, and husbands, in so much as they participate, are drawn into the orbit of their mothers-in-law because of the close mother–daughter relationship. Home in a traditional working-class area is a place on the whole almost exclusively reserved for family and kinsmen. Partly this exclusiveness is on account of cramped conditions, partly it is a legacy of the poverty of the past when families were sensitive and reluctant to expose their threadbare possessions and parsimonious contrivances to the prying eyes of gossiping neighbours. But a very large acquaintance meet in shops, streets, parks and pubs, because friends of all kin become friends or aquaintances of the whole group.

The texture of life in the middle class at the level of semi-detached suburbia as manifest in styles of entertaining, willingness to join clubs and so on, differs from that of the traditional working class, but the fabric has important features in common, particularly in the sphere of kinship interaction. In both there is more contact with the mother and her kin than with the father and his kin, but the middle-class daughter may have a closer relationship with her father than the traditional working-class daughter, and the middle-class mother is less of an authority figure than her traditional working-class counterpart. Although the middle-class mother–daughter relationship is also central, the two may not see one another so often because they are less likely to live in the immediate neighbourhood than are members of the working class in which the generations traditionally reside nearby all their lives; when they do, they too meet with great frequency. In middle-class Woodford, for example, it was found that of all the married women with mothers alive, two-thirds had seen them in the previous week, and only about one-fifth had not seen them for as much as a month before the survey interviews.

When the kingroup is geographically dispersed higher incomes give the middle class greater physical mobility which lessens the isolating effect of distance. Their higher incomes, too, open up a variety of other ways of keeping in touch, such as cultural or sporting interests and their usually more spacious houses enable them to have their relations to stay. More letters, photographs and Christmas cards are exchanged, and the telephone, still largely confined to middle-class households, has become an important way of maintaining contacts. Surveys report daily conversations between mothers and daughters which sometimes last for an hour, and husbands are reported to complain about rocketing bills for trunk calls. It appears, therefore, that kinship sentiment is stronger among the middle classes than has been supposed, even when face-to-face contacts are infrequent, and although meetings tend, as some of the evidence suggests, to be a little more formal and pre-arranged than in the working class, it seems that considerable efforts are made to keep in touch, even with rather remote connections.

But the ties are more than those of sentiment. Empirical investigations in the United States have shown that middle-class parents often give substantial financial aid to their married children in the form of regular allowances, costly presents and the like. Recent kinship studies in Britain have established that here, too, middle-class married couples at the family building stage not infrequently receive considerable and valuable tangible help from their parents in the form of expensive toys, clothes, cars and even houses which otherwise would be out of their reach and which are status-giving to them or their children. More interesting perhaps is the unravelling of the process of parental support. The channel of communication when financial help is given is typically father–son or father–son-in-law, depending on circumstances, and incidentally providing supporting evidence that the mother–daughter relationship, although of great importance, is not so overwhelmingly predominant in families at this level as it is in the traditional working class.[2] Direct help, it seems, is rarely requested by married children, but the broadest hints are dropped by the young husband and freely acted upon by the older man. Some delicacy or face-saving devices are usually employed so that the young couple do not feel beholden to their elders. A common practice is to give remarkably generous gifts for Christmas or birthdays, gifts which enhance appreciably the young couple's standard of living. It follows that in the status game those with middle-class origins have a head start over those of working-class parentage who achieve middle-class status by means of job success alone. The latter, it has been estimated, lag about two years [3] behind more fortunately placed contemporaries at the same occupational level in acquiring the appurtenances of glossy living.

In the Woodford study, which set out to compare family life in a moderately prosperous middle-class suburb with that in the traditional working-class district of Bethnal Green, it was found, surprisingly, that adult middle-class children lived at home with their parents as often as did their working-class contemporaries. It was found too, that there was a general desire among parents with growing families to live near enough to the grandparents to allow them to become well acquainted with their grandchildren, to be included in family celebrations and to lend a hand with the children occasionally. Help of a very practical kind was given to the elderly by their married children, who kept in touch as much as did the Bethnal Greeners, the only real difference being that in Bethnal Green there was often more than one married child available, in Woodford usually only one. In Woodford, as in Bethnal Green, the older and more feeble the aged became, the more intensive was the care given by the married children; in Woodford as many as 41 per cent of the elderly were living in the house of a married child.

The fact that the aged middle class join their children's households late in life, often in a district in which they have no roots and at a time when they are hampered by age from establishing them, results in a situation with incipient tensions. These are dealt with in various ways. Among the more prosperous middle class it is becoming increasingly common to allocate part of a house, preferably self-contained or a converted outhouse, to aged parents who are still reasonably self-sufficient; and this often seems to constitute a mutually satisfactory compromise, combining some real independence with support when needed. Others, less fortunately placed, simply share board and hearth (often the best bit) with varying degrees of good will.

How long this situation will continue in any social stratum is open to speculation. Recent research [4] has revealed the emergence of the four-generation family as a phenomenon of significance in our social structure in so far as it could alter this pattern of kinship interaction. Already, as a consequence partly of longer life expectancy, and partly of youthful marriage accompanied by early parenthood, 22 per cent of those over 65 in Britain are great-grandparents. If this trend gains momentum, the aged who look to their own children for care and company may well find that these children are past middle age, are themselves grandparents with obligations to their married children and grandchildren. It is feared that this situation will lead to a progressively greater isolation of the very old as time passes.

So it would seem that kinship networks are functional in our society in both the working and middle classes. A great deal of mutual helpfulness has been shown to exist in the form of reciprocal services. People apparently feel free to call on their kinsmen, even ones they do not much like, and indeed they *prefer* to do so rather than asking the help of friends or neighbours whom they may know much more intimately; and it is expected that some help will be forthcoming. Obligations relating to mutual supportiveness are thus recognised even if in some cases rather tenuously and reluctantly, but clearly proximity is a determining factor in translating the recognition of an obligation into action. So is the closeness of the group. In really close-knit groups, financial aid to widows, to pay off debts, or to start a business, is not uncommon, particularly when the group is set apart from the general community by religion or race, or is part of an immigrant or foreign community within the larger social structure. Such groups are distinguished by the fact that willingly or unwillingly they are united by cultural ties that are deviations from the cultural norms of the host society and which retain significance for them if only in peripheral ways. The extended kingroup assumes greater importance than our culture in general accords to it, and the functions associated with mutual supportiveness are much more evident than among most sectors of the native Anglo-Saxons who tend to limit financial help in particular to members of the nuclear family.

Economic co-operation of whatever kind reinforces kinship solidarity and is often a factor enhancing the cohesion of the more socially isolated groups. The Jews who fled from the pogroms in Russia at the end of the nineteenth century and provided the nucleus of the family-oriented tailoring trade in London's East End are one illustration. Among the London Italianates studied by Firth *et al.*, extended households were particularly noticeable among restaurateurs who apparently found in their kinsmen an abundant, cheap and reliable source of the necessary labour, as do Cypriots, Greeks and some orientals. Thus the work immigrants choose or which is available to them often supports their kinship organisation.

Among the native-born population the cohesive effect of economic co-operation on kinship interaction is at its most evident in rural conditions. A high proportion of farmers' sons still remain in farming, and many serve the paternal farm for part at least of their useful adult years. Wives typically have their own responsibilities outside the strictly domestic, which, depending on the area, may include poultry, pigs, vegetable garden and bookkeeping. Making a living is therefore a joint enterprise. Home and work are indivisible.

Rural social structure comprises family farms and their dependants cemented by a complicated network of intermarriage and kinship obligations. Farm families provide many reciprocal services for one another such as help with haymaking, sheep-shearing, the sharing of equipment, and services in time of trouble. These uncoded obligations are taken seriously and failure to fulfil them is severely sanctioned, occasionally by complete ostracism, a serious consequence when economic and social activities tend to merge, and most groups are kingroups. Businesses, too, in villages and country towns tend to be run by families, possessions and skills are handed down through the generations just as on the land, and they are also likely to have kinship ties with the surrounding farms. Common values permeate the whole complex, and the central one is consensus on the need for family continuity which manifests itself in filial piety and family loyalty. It is reinforced when property is involved and there are prospects of inheritance.

Property is an important factor influencing kinship solidarity, although it has a less general application in this respect in present-day Britain than it has had in other societies and at other times. Where it exists as in rural communities and among the upper classes, it makes for frequent contact between the generations, for apart from any motives of affection, those hoping to inherit wish to keep their prospects alive, and sometimes also to keep an eye on the hoped-for

4

bequest. But in general when social change is swift and society is open so that there are opportunities for advancement as a result of ability and effort, the sucession to property is less crucial than it is in more stable societies or in societies where social stratification is less flexible. Nevertheless, property and kinship solidarity are still linked.

Religion, too, reinforces kinship solidarity. In many societies elders in the family gain prestige by virtue of priestly duties and their offices as intermediaries with the gods, propitiators of the ancestral ghosts and so on. Religion is least likely to promote family cohesion when it amounts to no more than lip service to the established church for social or other secular reasons.

It may be concluded that the extended family and kingroup in Britain retain some importance in the economic sphere and as agents of social control, social support and social cohesion. But different social groups have their own way of life and the significance of kinship differs accordingly.

Neighbourhood

The life that is lived in the traditional working-class districts adjacent to the centres of the big cities, often in old dilapidated property in crowded sunless streets, has been described, somewhat fancifully perhaps, as being in all its essentials like that of a village. Some similarities there certainly are. Kinship networks extend longitudinally and collaterally, members perform reciprocal services, the aged have a recognised place in the structure and are cared for, and the group serves as an agent of social control in observing its own norms and those of the neighbourhood and of the community, except among the deviant groups. The central decaying areas of cities are the ones which are gradually being cleared, and rehousing programmes are breaking up the multi-generation matriarchal family and destroying city 'village' life.

A move to a dormitory estate brings dramatically changed conditions. Generously spaced houses with long front paths inhibit neighbourliness, and that amenities which might foster sociality are nearly always lacking on new estates, particularly early on, has been reiterated over and over for forty years. No longer is there a pub on almost every street corner, crowded, noisy, smoke-laden, intimate, its folkways well understood by its 'regulars'; and the glossy single substitute, perhaps half a mile or more from home, may at first seem a poor alien place. Shops with their streamlined interiors, and often grouped centrally in conformity with the aesthetic visual ideal of some planner, are not only expensive because of their near-monopoly conditions of trade, but again seem unfriendly places, far from many homes. In families with young children, the majority, shopping in such conditions calls for two or three well-planned forays weekly, whereas in the old city areas in which shops, often very small ones, are widely dispersed, it is possible to make odd purchases at the corner shop, aproned, feet in slippers and hair in rollers, a dozen times daily, to send children, so small they can hardly reach up to the counter, for errands, and most satisfying of all, to exchange news, gossip and generally keep in touch with other people's lives and the neighbourhood activities. Because of the generally spacious layout, schools, churches and the community centre, if there is one, are also considerable distances from all but the most favourably sited dwellings. Initially the adjustment required of the mother of a young family who for every trivial outing to shop or school must tidy herself, collect the children, clean them up and take the lot, is tremendous. And appearances matter, for no longer is she identified with a particular family whose reputation as 'respectable' (or the reverse!) is known throughout the neighbourhood. She and other newcomers like her are wary and may appear snobbish in the process of mutual appraisal, so she is diffident about making gestures which may be rebuffed, for in the kin-centred society from which she has been uprooted she will have had no experience of the institutionalised ways of contacting and judging neighbours on which middle-class suburbanites, many of them always on the move, rely in a similar situation. Bereft of the companionship of her mother and sisters, and from knowing everyone to knowing no one, her sheer immobility, the concomitant of motherhood, sharpens the isolation and loneliness.

The husband's way of life is also greatly modified. As there is usually little local industry, he typically stays in his old job and so sees his kinsmen and cronies, but it is not practicable to return to the old area after tea to pursue his old leisure pattern with his male contemporaries; it is too far and he is tired after his earlier start and later arrival home, and his wife, who may have spoken to no one over the age of five all day, is more demanding of his company. Money is initially very tight. From being only a short journey from work, fares are expensive. The rent is high and the splendid new house seems to demand splendid new furniture, so there may be over-commitment on hire purchase to provide visible symbols of the family's standing in alien territory. In addition the wife may have to stop working, if she has been doing so, because of a dearth of jobs locally and the loss of her female kin as minders. One way and another, husband and wife become more dependent on one another. The traditional pattern of men's and women's lives has disintegrated and as they are short of money, their lives of necessity become home-centred.

The social structure and texture of life on a new estate on the outskirts is a dramatic change for most, and many experience an acutely unsettled period. The length of the settling-in time depends to some extent on whether or not the move was compulsory or voluntary. It is also easier to go, not to a raw brand new estate, but to a settled community in which there are already some contacts from the old area, as happened to some of the later Bethnal Green *émigrés*. Recent but isolated experiments have been made in building new houses around existing social groups, but many local authorities give preference to outsiders in allocating vacant houses. It is not only the younger generation which is affected by this policy. The destruction of the multi-generation family structure deprives the old grandparents of a function in life, and the children of the considerable benefits of a close and often indulgent relationship with their grandparents. The problems of caring for the old and the young are therefore intensified. The tendency for the nuclear family to emerge as the most important social unit is underlined and the disappearance of the strong community spirit which still exists in old working-class neighbourhoods is accelerated. All these changes could have far-reaching effects, for a great number of studies appear to show that a sense of belonging to a living community is vital to thriving family life, and that the two elements which contribute most to this sense of belonging are long residence, and the presence of kin. If these conclusions are correct, then many of the plans suggested to alleviate the problems of living on a housing estate in its initial stages must be seen as what they are, no more than palliatives.

Once the barriers are down, however, a new pattern of life emerges which is characterised by relationships which have been called 'quasi-primary', that is somewhere between the intimacy of true primary relationships and the vigilance of secondary ones, a situation in which dependence is upon friends and neighbours rather than upon kin. With the father and schoolchildren out at midday the main meal is taken in the evening. With the chip shop less immediately available, the type of food served may be modified and diversified. There is more entertaining in the home. A middle-class value is put upon education which begins to be seen as an avenue of upward social mobility. Among those who prosper, refrigerators, washing machines, holidays and motor-cars burgeon. The number who can afford all these 'middle-class' amenities is small, but the aspiration to enjoy them is not as unrealistic as it was a generation ago.

It should be noted, however, that some sociologists currently argue that the alleged 'embourgeoisement' of working-class families is to some extent a myth and that the 'essential' working-class values and attitudes remain basically unaltered, either in new surroundings or by greater affluence.[5] This thesis is given support by studies such as the one at Dagenham,[6] a 'one-class' community, which showed that the working-class ethos can be maintained for many years. But the same conclusion may not follow if the community has or acquires greater heterogeneity.

Not all suburban living can be neatly docketed as working class or middle class, although English sociologists have tended to study suburban life by means of these categories with their main emphasis on the working class. Neither can the social consequences of removal to the outskirts always be explained largely in terms of house-type, low density, estate layout and spatial separation from kin and old associations. The tight social control of a close-knit neighbourhood is not necessarily lost in a move to the outskirts. A recent major study[7]

45

of social interaction in a prototypical American new town suggests that there it is the house which is the focal point in increasing joint family activity, not the neighbourhood, that the importance of layout in the creation of community spirit has been exaggerated, and that the social isolates have certain characteristics which are quite independent of their physical surroundings. Other old assumptions have been challenged or discredited, too. For example, not all men deplore the lack of employment on the doorstep, but some positively enjoy the camaraderie of the journey to work. A not inconsiderable number also appear to derive satisfaction from the inaccessibility of their mothers-in-law. The American investigators found little depressive illness or even boredom. On the contrary, social activities abounded and expressions of satisfaction with suburban life were the rule, and when evidence of severe stress or mental illness was found, it was frequently present before the move. Stress was experienced by the downwardly socially mobile, but this is a general phenomenon, not specific to suburbia. Many of those rising up the social ladder and always on the move also characteristically have identity problems. In other cases, the stress arose from isolation which was correlated with certain other variables which set the isolates apart. It would seem that those who suffer from social isolation differ in some way such as age, educational or social level from the majority of their neighbours. But among those who fitted into the 'normal' pattern, the incidence of stress decreased.

There is a flourishing social life on many types of housing estate after the initial settling-in period has been weathered, provided income is adequate to subscribe to the cultural norms and personal values are in line with the prescribed mores; for when families participate in local organisations and institutions, as they almost must, (for the relationship between family and community, if only through the school, is crucial to the development of individual family members in modern society), they are wholly at ease only when these institutions reflect accurately values upheld by the family. Diversity of values then is a complicating factor and a source of conflict, although it is also a potential source of richness in community life.

Another well-worn belief which may also be suspect is the breakdown of standards on release from the social controls of the old neighbourhoods. American evidence indicates that conventional morality is strictly adhered to. It cannot of course be lightly assumed that American evidence is valid for Britain. But suburbs have certain characteristics in common in all complex societies, and common sense suggests that we re-examine our own beliefs in the light of American findings. Why should it be assumed that a generation which has abandoned the cloth cap and muffler should yearn for the sawdust and spittoons of the old pubs? And does it not seem likely that when the picture in one's picture window is through the neighbour's picture window, it is not coincidence that a strict monogamy often prevails in such a neighbourhood? Adultery is easier in more secluded dwellings or in the anonymity of some areas of the city, as are other social deviations.

Both English and American sociologists have identified homogeneity as a principal determinant of social interaction by showing that different patterns of sociability emerge in otherwise identical housing developments according to whether they are occupied by homogeneous or heterogeneous groups, and this seems to be so whatever the density or type of housing layout. But class, so dominant in many studies, is only one type of homogeneity; age can also be a potent factor in promoting social interaction. Young families tend to predominate in municipal suburbia when housing is allocated on a 'points' system which gives priority to those with young children, and young couples with children are also those principally attracted to privately financed suburban housing developments. So new estates have much else in common besides class, and particularly demographic structure, composition of household and income. And these factors can characterise an estate even when the class and life style of some of the residents differ, the case in Levittown as when, for example, the rising young executive with far to go lives next door to the young technician with a similar current income but who has reached his occupational peak early in life. Once houses begin to change hands, however, heterogeneity starts to creep in. In these circumstances neighbourhoods often cease to cohere, a process readily observable in decaying middle-class areas. Conversely it should be noted that the age of an area determines its demographic structure and the types of families which live in it. Thus there is no one sub-urban way of life; it is only certain characteristics which different suburbs have in common such as low-density, single-family dwellings, gardens and relative absence of industry. But they differ one from another in important ways such as income level, age and type of housing, degree of homogeneity, demographic structure, and also in relation to the characteristics of nearby areas.

It has been shown that when new hypotheses are investigated old ones frequently become suspect or invalid, so conclusions about the effects of suburbia on family life can only be tentative. With aspirations for home ownership becoming pervasive and more realistic, with the decline in the amount of privately-owned centrally-situated rented property available, and with the removal of city dwellers to subsidised peripheral estates, an understanding of the processes of suburban living is of current importance. We know that real problems are created for overworked young mothers cut off from their kin. On the other hand suburbia provides a relatively sheltered and healthy environment for children, and conditions favourable to socialisation inhibit family disintegration. Nuclear family members, too, are more involved with one another and with the home itself, and in these ways suburban life may be said to have positive effects on family cohesion.

Part II

Some small group aspects

The family is not only a component part of a larger social structure. It has itself a degree of wholeness or completeness and some sociologists choose to view it in terms of *small group* structure, as 'a unity of interacting personalities' to use E. W. Burgess's well-worn and now classic phrase.

The intimacy of the family group and its continuity have importance in supplying a sense of security and well-being for the individual member. In the family setting he finds a secure base which enhances his sense of identity and from which he can savour and appraise new experience. The giving and receiving of affection, and the acceptance of the family member for himself, provide scope for individual personality development. In fact, the family fulfils all the needs of the individual that can be met by other primary groups such as clubs, friendship groups or work groups, and it does so with a greater degree of permanency than do most others, the composition of which changes as lives alter. Emotional security and gratification within the family compensate for the trials and anxieties of modern life, for the competitiveness and impersonality of many external relationships, all of which may be sources of feelings of personal insecurity and of inner conflict. The family hearth has become an oasis or retreat, cushioned against outside pressures and within which individuality may be cultivated. In our own society all these 'psychological functions', as they have been called, are rated highly, and the needs of the group itself no longer necessarily take precedence over individual needs as was often the case in the past.

On the whole, in the eyes of the outside world all family members enjoy the same or similar status, that is, the ascribed status which comes of membership of an involuntary association. But there is a status hierarchy within the family group itself. The status of the individual family member will be indicated by the privileges he is accorded and by the types of behaviour permitted to him. It will be dependent on what he contributes actually or potentially to the family's welfare. In less complex societies the old gained status because they were considered wise; age in our society brings little status, for wisdom has been dethroned by technological know-how, which is largely the prerogative of the young. Property confers status regardless of age. Some statuses within the family are achieved from attainment outside the immediate group, from the esteem of others in the community; for familial and societal values interlock. In the contemporary family even the receipt of love, affection, acceptance, and emotional support are thus linked in some degree with external 'success'.

There are many statuses within a family group, and in association with each status there is a recognised and institutionalised role to be played. There are also expectations of how it will be played attached to each role; and as the appropriate behaviour in each role is in accordance with a set of norms, it follows that a set of reciprocal relationships are also normatively prescribed. It is possible, therefore, to view family structure in terms of *statuses and roles*, a perspective currently popular among sociologists, although it should be noted that this is only *one* of the perspectives from which family structure can be studied.

Each individual in a family group also has a number of statuses and similarly in each of them his behaviour is influenced by the expectations attaching to the role. For example, a man may be a husband, father, son, brother, breadwinner and so on, and he plays the appropriate roles for each of his statuses. If he misinterprets his roles, plays them inadequately or misguidedly, or evades playing them in so far as he can, then strains and tension will result. Conversely, if he faces up to his roles and plays them adequately then the chances of the development of well-adjusted relationships are much enhanced. In other words there are expectations attached to roles both by those fulfilling them and by others. The limits of these role expectations will be largely defined in terms of geographical location, age, sex, class-status position in society, educational level and occupation. The boundaries are thus set within which a family group will act.

A family member also has a number of extra-familial statuses, as for example, trade union member, stock breeder and so on, and the ways in which he plays the roles attached to his extra-familial statuses also affect his internal family relationships. If a number of conflicting loyalties call for reconciliation, *role strain* or even *role conflict* may follow unless the resulting tensions are resolved. For example, when the role expectation of the wife–mother is primarily that of homemaker, role strain may become evident if she undertakes civic duties, or joins clubs, or takes a job; or it may be, to give another example, that opportunities for personal advancement are offered to children which are difficult to reconcile with family obligations to elderly parents. Family loyalties frequently conflict with other duties or preferences. In modern societies, too, family members may be constrained to concede prior claim to organisations outside the family such as the state with its demand for taxation and military service, or the business concern which indirectly but relentlessly may determine the way of life of its employees.

In highly complex and industrialised societies such as our own, in which the family performs minimal functions and in which the close-knit nuclear family unit relatively isolated from the wider kingroup tends to predominate, roles are flexible and the family is able to adapt to outside situations. There are also fewer roles than there were, or are, in more functional or extended families. The principal family statuses of father, mother, son and daughter, all have less importance in nuclear families than they do in highly functional families. In the latter, role relationships tend to be complicated but well defined, and individuals have little freedom to act independently in the pursuit of their personal goals. When roles are indistinct, when there is little general agreement on the allocation of tasks and responsibilities, which tends to be the position in the now pervasive nuclear family, the norms governing the relationships within the family also become confused.

Differentiation of sex roles

Men and women in any society have roles which are defined. To use the terminology popularised by Zelditch and the Parsonians, the masculine role tends to be *instrumental* and the feminine role to be *expressive*.[1] Both the instrumental and the expressive roles appear necessary for a satisfactory family environment, and a clear definition of sex roles on instrumental and expressive lines contributes, the Parsonians argue, to the maintenance of the nuclear family as a stable social 'system'.

Role allocation differs between societies, but the range of variation has limits, for it rests principally on the differentiation of function between the sexes. Of fundamental importance in the allocation of roles, even in modern societies, is the initial biological closeness between mother and child, which makes it convenient and logical for the mother to concentrate on the expressive family roles, that is to become the focus of warmth and affection, and to symbolise the integration of the family. The mother, because of her biological functions, is also relatively immobile, so it happens that men tend to take on the instrumental roles, which require a degree of physical mobility, the roles of breadwinning, organising and leadership, in particular. The authority given by the successful performance of these roles and the absence and comparative remoteness consequent upon them have in addition often made it appropriate for the father to take on responsibility for discipline. Furthermore, in so far as the mother's role is one of warmth and comforting, the child has first of all to be weaned from over-dependency on his mother and then persuaded, or compelled, to learn the appropriate societal behaviour. These are to some extent matters of discipline, which the father is the parent best placed to provide. Similarly, the mother's position, because she is, in the early years, most fully available, is best adapted to fulfil the expressive roles.

In all societies, too, strength and physical fitness are important determinants of role differentiation within the family, although in particular families, at certain levels of development, other factors may have priority such as intelligence or special talents. But, other things being equal, those who are strongest take on most roles and, as a multiplicity of roles confers prestige, authority is likely to accumulate in male hands unless there are other countervailing influences at work to modify this tendency. In contemporary society male roles are not only more in number but are less often family centred, which also confers prestige, provided they are played successfully. To the individual man it may well be that, in some cases, his extra-familial roles are those which have most meaning for him. And the man gains status within the family, that is masculine roles are more highly regarded than feminine ones, even within the family unit, because he has, or seems to have, power in the wider society. Even the least prepossessing of men acquire some aura simply by virtue of their participation in a mysterious male world separate from family life. However, as women too may now lead a life independent of the family, this source of male status is evaporating. Property is also often in the hands of men, although less frequently now than in the past, and they also derive power and authority from their relationship to it.

Basically the distinction between the masculine instrumental roles and the feminine expressive roles remains in western societies where men, with few exceptions, leave home to perform the role of bread-winning. The distinction is in some circumstances intensified [2] when the man commutes long distances and the woman remains at home in a nuclear group isolated from the wider kingroup. Maleness of itself no longer confers status automatically as in the past. 'Breadwinner' is often no less than the true appraisal of his role—he may be literally this and no more—and if his wife is also earning, he is only part breadwinner at that. Or his self-confidence may be undermined in a female ascendant household; the father in mother-centred families often has little real authority with which to play out his expected role as head of the household. Indeed, industrial-urban conditions are not such as to maximise male authority. Male authority is greatest where onerous responsibilities are shouldered, where the man is the policy-maker and work allocator as on the farm or in a family business. He also gains status from superior physical strength when this can be used in work, or in protecting his family from dangers be it from wolves or from maurauding tribesmen. He has status in a society dominated by ancestor worship or in any situation where a leader or figurehead is an essential of the social structure. In a modern family he will have more status if he is the only wage earner, the sole support of his wife and children, rather than when they too contribute to the family income by their earnings.

In our own and in many other societies, the distinction which was formerly well defined between masculine and feminine roles has in general become blurred, but the separation of roles remains more defined in some classes and in some situations than it does in others; and differing patterns of authority are expressions of different value systems, and the value systems are a reflection of the social structures in which they are found.

All these inter-related factors, together with the degree and type of economic development, have significance for the division of labour between the sexes, or *task-allocation* as the Americans call it. Furthermore, the form this division of labour takes has significance, not only for the family as a social system, but also for the distribution of authority and the balance of power within the family, and hence on its more intimate personal relationships.

Male role and participation in family life

The contemporary marriage ethos prescribes that marriage is an equal partnership in which husband and wife share their lives and the responsibility for major decisions in consultation, and the acceptance of such ideals is a factor contributing towards a blurring of the former distinction between men's and women's familial tasks. The man at the sink need no longer be furtive and downcast. He has ceased to be a figure of fun and become a fact of life. He is quite likely to be applauded. He is certainly socially approved. Manuals on family living illustrate smiling, aproned husbands and wives together in the kitchen with captions such as 'you can have fun at the sink'. Sociologists make seriously intended and expensive comparative studies of male dishwashing practice in Scandinavia and the United States. It seems that many fathers now participate very fully in domestic and child-rearing activities. The Newsoms' Nottingham survey showed that 79 per cent of the sample mothers received or could call on substantial help from their husbands in caring for their babies.[3] Other surveys suggest that over half the husbands of working wives give some help at home.

The change has affected many social strata. In the middle class some attitudes survive that derive from the expectation, now unfulfilled, of cheap domestic help,[4] but there can be few middle-class households left where the husband, and other male members of the family, are not 'allowed' into the kitchen (a convention founded on the fear that the servants would be 'upset' or seduced), a situation not uncommon in the last generation. Middle-class wives, it seems, now take all the help they are offered, from any source, paid or unpaid. No doubt there are still men at other social levels who regard looking after the house and children as women's work and who participate minimally. An extreme example is the Nottingham wife quoted as saying:

He does just look after them on Saturday afternoon, that's when I do my shopping—he just lies there on the sofa . . . lets them do whatever they like, just lets them get on with it. I *suppose* he'd stop them falling in the fire. Oh— you should have seen them when I got in last week! They'd got a packet of cornflakes and a packet of sugar out of the cupboard, and they'd emptied them out here all over the mat, and they were digging in it. And he just lay there.[5]

It seems that it is only a small minority of fathers who now evade all participation and few with such deliberate disinterestedness as the example quoted, but that patterns of male participation may vary in accordance with socio-economic factors. The father's occupation and hours of work are important. Small independent businessmen, resident in or near their place of work, tend to be highly participant; so do shift workers who are likely to be at home for at least some of their children's waking hours and to have few male distractions since most other men are at work. Occupation effectively excludes the father from active regular participation if it takes him much away from home as happens with for example seafarers, lorry drivers, and some businessmen. When the man works, say, a 40-hour week at a job

5

which is neither physically nor intellectually exacting, as many do, it is evident that his help will enable his wife to take greater pleasure in her family life, to the benefit of all. On the other hand, where the male need for job success (deeply rooted in our society) in highly competitive conditions is a dominant factor, the expectation that he should help at home may impose almost intolerable strains on the husband, impair his efficiency at work and hence his self-esteem.

Not all types of family either live up to or accept the emergent ideal of equal, mutually shared responsibilities between the marriage partners, including the domestic work. The traditional working-class family is still characterised to a greater or lesser degree by strict role and task allocation between the sexes. The ideal wife is patient, submissive, home-centred and self-effacing where her husband's interests are concerned. There is no expectation that marriage should be a partnership of equals; rather it is viewed as a contract with a strict definition of masculine and feminine roles, together with an equally strict allocation of male and female tasks, and a good marriage is one in which both spouses carry out their recognised obligations. The man is the breadwinner, the woman looks after the house and the children, and ministers to the needs of her husband and of the other adult males, if there are any, and the convention that she should work only in the home is reinforced when there is a shortage of outside employment suited to the housewife available, which is often the case in areas mainly dependent on mining or heavy industries. Family life is dominated by the arduous nature of the man's job and the wife ensures that he has nourishing food, undisturbed rest and recreation to refresh him and enable him to face the labours ahead. Typically, this means in practice that the wife's activities are defined strictly in terms of the husband's convenience;[6] that he eats the moment he arrives home and is given the best food available, particularly the meat and savoury dishes. The wife and children usually eat when the men are out, and if food is short, it is the mother who goes without. Both spouses take it for granted that this is proper, and also that he should have generous spending money. Husband and wife have few interests in common; their lives are different and separate. The strict definition of masculine and feminine roles is emphasised early. Boys are made much of, and girls are expected to defer to boys and to share household duties with their mothers from an early age, which the boys never do.

Despite the matriarchal kinship structure, the husband usually has a dominant position in so far as he keeps control over his earnings, and this is accepted. It seems that many still do not tell their wives how much they earn and retain a disproportionately large sum for their own pleasures. From what remains, the wife will pay for rent, fuel, food, clothes and all household necessities, and she may receive no increase in her allowance as expenses or wages rise. In some northern communities, on the other hand, it is common for the man to hand over his unopened wage packet to his wife, and, ironically, this tends to happen in areas in which there is a tradition of women's employment outside the home (women have always worked in the mills of Lancashire and Yorkshire, for example). That traditional working-class family life has been considerably modified as a consequence of the increasing habit of married women working outside the home, among other factors, has been amply brought out in various studies. But that the harsh traditional pattern lingers on, albeit in a somewhat modified form, is also evident, even with the advent of greater economic security and higher real incomes. Although an independent income enhances a woman's status, in some areas her role is modified only slightly and slowly in the face of old outworn attitudes. She may still, for example, be expected to do *all* the housework, and in such cases she may be as hard put to it to provide proper standards as in the past when money was much scarcer, for she will perforce be driven or tempted to use expensive ready-prepared, quickly-heated-up food which gives less satisfaction in food value, quality or flavour, shilling for shilling spent.

Nevertheless, as masculine and feminine roles cease to be clear-cut, as men do less exhausting work for shorter hours, men tend to give more help with the traditionally female activities. Sometimes, however, these very factors may operate to reinforce the traditional pattern of male dominance. In jobs where work and home are not too separate, or where the father is frequently at home when the children are about, there is evidence to show that he remains the dominant and dominating authority figure, even in a modern industrial setting. He becomes highly participant in all aspects of family life, and frequent decision-taking even on small issues, impossible for the long-distance commuter, correlates with high authority. The oft-expressed current view that high male participation necessarily denotes a lack of male authority needs re-examination. It is only valid in some situations.

There could be some disadvantages in too easy an interchange of roles between young parents. Children, it has been suggested, may find it difficult to identify as male or female, and this may hinder their development if, in effect, they have two mothers as a consequence of the father's very full participation in caring for them. As against the possible risks of this situation, which have been hypothesised but not proven, the physical and emotional strains on the mother running a household containing young children single-handed must be calculated.

The changing feminine role

As we have seen, when roles are indistinct the norms governing relationships within the family become confused. Women have now achieved full adult status in the legal sense, together with the rights which accompany it. Enfranchisement has accorded political status. The establishment of academically sound girls' schools in the nineteenth century made entrance to the universities feasible for women and hence admission to the professions also, with the later consequence that all women have achieved 'the right to work', and opportunities for economic independence, opened up by the Married Women's Property Acts, 1880–82, which removed disabilities in relation to property ownership, have thus been consolidated. All these changes in status have come about within a century and they are associated with changes in and indecisiveness about feminine roles in the family and in society itself.

Of all the changes which have occurred in the last few decades, the growing practice of married women working outside the home has received the most attention. Indeed, the working wife, because of her impact as a contemporary social phenomenon, and because of the amount of research she has attracted is, in at least one work of reference, elevated to the status of a sociological concept. Despite continuing and often tedious polemics, for many women the feminine role is no longer either that of home-maker *or* wage earner, but of both, at least for part of their married lives, and because women do not act in a vacuum, men's roles and statuses have been modified also.

Of the many factors which influence the incidence of wives who work outside the home, some are societal in origin and some are personal. There is an interdependence between the two, for personal reasons react to the social, political and economic climate of the times.

For example married women's work was strenuously discouraged in Nazi Germany with the objective of checking a declining birth rate which at that time was becoming a threat to the fatherland's military potential. Motherhood was exalted and reverenced; women were urged back to the home and exhorted to centre their lives on *Kirche*, *Kinder* and *Küche*. They were indeed given concrete incentives to do so in the form of loans (a quarter was cancelled on the birth of each child), preferential treatment of families in the allocation of subsidised housing, and other privileges. The state of the economy also has relevance. In periods of economic depression, married women are unwelcome competitors for scarce jobs, resented, as they were in the early thirties, by both men and single women. But for most of the years since the Second World War, with the exceptions of a few industries and areas, the demand for labour in Britain has exceeded the supply. The shortage has been intensified by the raising of the school leaving age, and by the opening up of educational opportunities to embrace wider social ranges, all of which have combined to denude the labour market of juveniles. One way and another the economy depends heavily on women's labour and increasingly on that of married women, who now comprise the only and diminishing reserve pool. The position could be reversed by mounting unemployment or a marked trade recession. But for the moment the drift out of the home is an established trend, reinforced by the current taste for early marriage which is necessarily accompanied by a contraction in the number of young spinsters potentially available to the economy.

Another social factor which has contributed to the readiness of women to work outside the home is the general increase in leisure consequent upon the development of technology and automation.[1] Domestic appliances and gadgets reduce the amount of fatigue in routine household tasks and also the time needed to complete them. Synthetic fibres have revolutionised the care of clothes and linen, all but eliminating boiling, starching, ironing and mending. Preserving, baking and stoking open fires are frequently avoided altogether in modern homes which, together with the smaller size of families, makes household organisation less than a full-time occupation for many. Furthermore patterns of family building have changed. Active motherhood is over early, so that the last child in a family may have reached school age long before his mother is 40, which, at a time when life expectancy is increasing, may well leave her with at least as much time again to fill up.

A wife's or mother's attitude to taking a job will be influenced by her educational background and by class and neighbourhood norms. Taking all social levels into account, wives with higher education or occupational qualifications are those most likely to work after marriage [2] and the higher the academic or professional standing the greater the likelihood. Graduates with a second or third degree are more likely to have jobs than those with only one. Of these married women, teachers, doctors and dentists work in the highest proportions. The intrinsic interest of their jobs is evident, the pattern of work or a return to work is accepted and, significantly, many of them are married to those in the same professions. But at this level there are powerful financial disincentives. Many additional expenses derive from a job. Extra domestic help and the sole use of a second family car are regarded as essential by the woman at this level as surveys show, and even clothes are considerable expense; not for her an ancient pair of slacks, the current badge of office for those who work only around house and garden. Although in an increasingly complex age, technologically and otherwise, the supply of qualified people tends to lag behind the number of jobs available so that the well-qualified woman may be fairly highly paid, the tax laws are unfavourable and indeed almost punitive, for a married woman's income is tacked on to that of her husband for tax purposes. In so far as able women tend to marry able men (like tends to marry like, as we shall see), and as able men are more likely to reach the surtax-paying class than others, it follows that such women *must* earn substantially if it is to be worth their while at all. The less educated wives of surtax-paying husbands, significantly, tend to remain domestic. So do those whose services are in demand, but are relatively poorly paid, such as nurses.

It is not long ago that it was still against middle-class mores that women should be 'too highly' educated or that wives should work. These attitudes still linger and there are more cultural deterrents for some who might consider taking up the 'self-inflicted burden' of paid employment than there are for others. In some circles in which wives by means of their conspicuous consumption and idle lives display the success of their husband's business acumen and the extent of his resources, a loss of status may accrue. Nevertheless, status is accorded generally in relation to economic activity, and in all types of societies, simple and complex, women tend to be respected when they are economically useful or indispensable. Increasingly in modern societies a wife's earnings can add to her own status provided they are procured by work which does not entail a 'loss of caste'. For the middle class, the acceptable ways of earning, part- or full-time, are in the professions, in the arts as an executant, and in journalism, of which there are examples in high places such as the late Mrs Eleanor Roosevelt, as well as the bright young marrieds in Britain whose astringent copy on everything from maternities to investments crowds out the news from some of our newspapers. 'Business' may also add status, but there are reservations here. Retail trade, except for the ownership and direction of sizeable and successful enterprises, would tend to detract from the middle-class wife's status at the upper levels, as would any connection with distribution or service occupations. The same considerations would not apply in rather lower socio-economic strata where the additional income alone, and the consumer goods it could buy, would tend to enhance the status not only of the wife but of the whole family. This is particularly so at the upper levels of the working class, in which relatively large numbers of wives also work compared with other social strata, and whose earnings may bring house-ownership nearer, or holidays in the sun or a motor-car, aspirations which could not even have been entertained in the insecurity of pre-war economic conditions.

Although socio-economic conditions have been favourable to married women's work since the war, this does not mean that every wife can find a job which enables her to perform optimally the double role of home-maker and wage earner. There are regional variations. It will be relatively easy in areas or industries where there is a tradition of wives working, for example in textiles where married women's work in the mills has long been accepted and does not arouse hostility. But in districts where unemployment is above the average, and also in areas dominated by heavy industries for which muscular strength is at a premium, the competition for female jobs is likely to be keen. When an area is dependent on one or two industries, there may be little choice. Rural women, too, are at a disadvantage. If they have a choice of jobs at all it is from a limited range only, and they are handicapped further by a lack of services, such as laundries or bread deliveries, which townswomen take for granted.

The personal considerations, as distinct from societal pressures, which influence an individual wife's willingness to take a job will include the availability of such services. Not all are provided adequately even in the towns. Day nurseries, for example, have long waiting lists and cater for about one-quarter only of the estimated need, and they exclude the children of part-time workers altogether. Individual decisions to work outside the home are crucially affected by the problem of providing adequate care for children. Half the married women at work have children under school leaving age, but difficulties are most acute when children are under school age. Changing demographic structure and rehousing schemes have restricted the availability of grandmothers who are regarded by many health visitors and others as the most satisfactory minders of young children because of their personal emotional involvement. But the youthful grandmothers of today are frequently at work themselves or they may be left behind in the decaying central areas of a city. It has been suggested on evidence from survey material that about one-third of working mothers' children under 5 could be receiving 'care' which is seriously substandard.[3]

Most surveys of working wives produce evidence to show that when the mothers of very young children (0–3 years) go out to work there are severe economic pressures involved in a very high proportion of cases. Money seems to be an important motivation for most wives who work, whatever the ages of their children, and this is so even among those who do not work altogether from necessity as widows, divorcees or those with incapacitated husbands usually do. And it is clear that the financial inducements beckon beguilingly at every social and occupational level, and that even sheer cupidity plays a part in the craving for 'extras'. However, as children grow older and husbands more prosperous, other factors are increasingly involved such as a desire for company, the boredom of household routines, the interest of a job (a reason given by graduates as the principal one more often than money), and among those with scarce skills, the duty not to waste an expensive training. But such reasons are often secondary to the financial motivation and may even be rationalisations of it. Interesting, too, is that few working wives are conventional feminists, few express interest in 'the right to work', although several surveys show that a job, once embarked on, may give a sense of independence which is often relished.

Certainly it is practical rather than ideological considerations which are decisive. This is reflected in the ages of the wives who work. The lowest proportion is to be found in the 25–29 years old group, that is at the time when family building is at its zenith. Thereafter follows a steady increase in the proportions of each age group at work, until a peak is reached in the 45–49 age group. Then follows a falling-off as financial commitments in an emptying nest are less pressing, or husbands become prosperous, or health begins to fail. In all social groups there is an influx of mothers on to the labour market at the time the youngest child goes to school.

Husband's attitudes to working wives are changing. The approval and encouragement of husbands who are co-operative and interested contribute greatly to the successful integration of home and work. The hostility of the husband is among the most powerful deterrents at every social level. At almost every social level, too, elaborate contrivance of one kind or another is usually necessary to enable a mother to go out to work, even when her children are of school age. So is an ability to tolerate a variety of frustrations. Wives are tied to the area in which their husbands work, and for the geographically immobile, already at a disadvantage in the search for rewarding work because of lack of training or of schemes for re-training, it is not easy to find the right job with the right hours. Nursery and primary school hours do not suit full-time working mothers and supervision in the school holidays is a constant worry, again at every social level. Not surprisingly there is a marked preference for part-time work among all mothers, but there is a scarcity of part-time jobs and particularly of those with convenient hours, although there are some available, for example, for teachers, domestic cleaners, and lunch-time waitresses. Occasionally factories run 10 a.m.–4 p.m. shifts which are highly successful, but on the whole there is a reluctance in industry, primarily interested in the mother's output rather than in the welfare of her children except in so far as it affects production, to modify hours of work or to make any concessions which could be resented by other women workers or which would increase overhead costs. One consequence is that mothers with heavy responsibilities at home tend to turn their full-time jobs into part-time jobs by taking time off more or less regularly for shopping or to catch up on the domestic back-log. Rarely, too, do mothers for long put the demands of a job before the needs of a sick child, which is one reason why they tend to drift in and out of jobs and to work spasmodically, but older women, whose children have left home or are at self-sufficient ages, have been shown to be loyal and effective workers with a low labour turnover, both in industry and elsewhere. Nevertheless, motherhood and the lack of geographical mobility it entails often impedes a woman's chances of promotion and she may, therefore, find herself in middle age with only junior status in her occupation.

Effects on children and on family life

Working wives and mothers are only one aspect of a complex pattern of social changes and cannot be treated in isolation without distortion. It is impossible at present to say, for example, which facets of the changed lives of families are causally connected with mothers at work and which with greater affluence, materialist values, exposure to mass media, changes in educational opportunities and so on. The internal structure of the family is another variable affecting the child; the composition of the household, the number, spacing and sexes of the children, the degree of marital harmony, of emotional and financial security, the educational level of the parents, all are important. So are the family environment, the cultural norms of the neighbourhood, the school and its teachers and other pupils.

A very bleak picture is often painted of the children of working mothers by teachers, school welfare officers, magistrates, health visitors, clergy and others, who represent them as neglected physically and emotionally, a picture which is itself dependent on *ex cathedra* pronouncements in accordance with a set of beliefs rather than on a cool appraisal of the total situation. Sentiment prescribes that a mother should be a 'real' home-maker and that this is a full-time job. Material values are being allowed to predominate, we are told, to the exclusion of others more commendable. Money is not everything, and material goods are no substitute for emotional security, as if the two were necessarily incompatible. Affluence carries other disadvantages; for instance, children have too much pocket money and are not taught the virtue of thrift. The mothers of these little spendthrifts are depicted as chronically cross, tired, irritable, preoccupied with catching up on their neglected housework and, when not reaching for the tin-opener, as feeding the family on extravagant fried foods which are quick and simple to prepare. Just wherein lies the virtue in spending long hours on kitchen work or anything else unnecessarily, or in *not* taking advantage of living in a technological century, is never made clear. Neither is the assumption ever substantiated that it is the wholly domesticated with their more restricted resources who produce the most interesting and nutritive food. Any reader of the glossy magazines knows that it is often the busiest women, actresses, journalists, and the like, who produce the most imaginative ideas for menus and indeed for home-making generally.

Nevertheless, recent evidence has revealed that quite large numbers [4] of children are frequently or always left unsupervised for an hour or two after school and also for the whole or most of the school holidays. The extent to which such children suffer physical or emotional neglect will depend upon their ages, temperaments, the proximity of relatives and on the ethos of the neighbourhood (some neighbourhoods have a sense of collective responsibility for their children). However, even when a mother makes arrangements for her child which on the surface appear satisfactory, the obvious pressures of her double role may make her less sensitive to her child's needs, unable or even unwilling to notice signs of latent stress. A number of comparative studies have been made to clarify the situation. On balance the evidence suggests that the children of working mothers show no more signs of stress than do other children, and that the records of the children of working mothers may even be rather better. If they go to hospital, they may stay there somewhat longer, but this could in part be a matter of convenience. It is arguable that the health of the children of working mothers may even be rather better than average; nearly half the mothers in one survey declared they had never had to cope with a child's illness. Certainly they have been shown to make good use of clinics and the health service as a whole. The evidence on intellectual development is in some respects contradictory. On the whole the children of working mothers appear to have better than average results at 11+. At ages up to eight there is some evidence to suggest that the children of non-working mothers make better progress at school.

There have been many attempts to establish a causal relationship between married women's work and juvenile delinquency, or with truancy which is often the forerunner of actual delinquency. Barbara Wootton [5] in a comprehensive résumé of the relevant literature could find little evidence, which would stand scrutiny, of a causal relationship between working mothers and juvenile delinquency. Her conclusion was that the amount of supervision and the type of discipline *are* relevant to the amount of delinquency, but that neither is *necessarily* absent in the working mother's home. Neither has direct evidence of a causal relationship been found in more recent studies. Inferences drawn from indirect evidence also lead to the same conclusion; there is nothing to suggest that in the past juvenile delinquency was any greater in the textile districts of Lancashire and Yorkshire, where there has been a long tradition of married women's work, than it was elsewhere. Today it is established that a large proportion of juvenile delinquents (i.e. those whose offences are recorded by the police) come from the most socially and economically deprived sectors of society. It is also known that the most socially depressed mothers are too burdened to go out to work regularly; for these are the mothers who often have large families, who themselves suffer chronic ill health, or whose husbands tend to be feckless, unemployable or perhaps in and out of gaol. The women who most frequently go out to work are the highly educated and those from the upper strata of the working class and the lowest stratum of the middle class; these particular social strata do not provide the bulk of juvenile delinquents. It must be remembered that the aetiology of delinquency includes many variables such as neglect, social isolation, parental friction, inconsistent discipline, or exposure to the norms of a delinquent sub-culture, to mention only a few of the possibly correlated factors, and as there is no general agreement on their relative significance, working mothers cannot logically be treated as a causative factor in isolation from the other possible variables.

The whole topic of the effects of mothers' and wives' employment outside the home is clearly emotive. Many writers have pointed to its 'beneficial' aspects. The financial benefits are not to be despised. Social investigators, moralists and others in comfortable circumstances, reprieved from or never having experienced life where 'every penny matters', may underestimate the emotional impoverishment which can derive directly from grossly inadequate material standards. And relative material deprivation is perhaps more acutely felt in times of good communication, when the affluence of others is paraded on the television screen, and the advertisers' insistence on one's right to cosset oneself ricochets across the tattered hearth rug. Money sensibly used can mean a fuller life.

Another viewpoint, again on inadequate evidence, stresses the gains of children who achieve independence to live their own lives and to take responsibility at an early age. They are much more capable than they are usually given the chance to show, it is argued. Such may be the case, but care is needed in pursuing this line of thought. The whole point of the early factory legislation, and of the increasingly elaborate structure of child welfare services, has been to enable children to flower in reasonably sheltered conditions and to protect them from many ingenious kinds of exploitation. Leaving them to fend for themselves at unsuitable stages of development can also be a form of exploiting children for the benefit of parents and employers. The children, the argument continues, will develop better in other ways. They will have a more interesting, stimulating mother, who is abreast of trends in the outside world, and whose advice is accordingly realistic. She is likely to be less possessive and more amenable to 'letting go' when children are adolescent. This is not proven either. If she is made to feel guilty she is quite as likely to become possessive and over-protective. Her job may even be deadening and make her *duller* company.

Many working wives claim that family relationships generally and the marriage relationship in particular are enriched. As husbands are almost inevitably more involved with domestic matters and in caring for the children it could well be that more common interests develop and a greater sense of partnership evolves as a concomitant of joint effort towards a common goal, as some women maintain. It is of course possible that these are the more energetic and vocal women, and that their sometimes clamorous insistence is symptomatic of their own doubts. Furthermore social expectations of the wifely role vary, and the egalitarian marriage is not yet fully established. Middle-class values, for example, still demand that the husband–father should be the 'provider', so there are likely to be conflicts in many households before a new pattern is accepted, particularly if it entails some erosion of the standards of comfort he expects. Ironically, it is a last ditch stand to maintain those same now largely outmoded standards which is sometimes the precipitating factor determining the more educated woman's decision to work. Nevertheless, a transitional phase seems to be firmly under way but, until it is weathered, husbands are likely to be irresolute about their own as well as their wives' roles as they become less clear cut than they were in the past, when the affirmation 'he is a good provider' was the highest compliment that could be made. When his wife is earning, the gradual destruction of the self-esteem which formerly accrued to the successful performance of the role of provider must result in inner conflicts. If he is not fulfilling the role expectations of the neighbourhood, whether through inability or not, it may seem that way to his peers, who have wives perhaps less educated, less gifted or less enterprising or energetic.

A priori arguments from unvalidated assumptions do not advance our knowledge, so it should be noted that many, if not most, of those who engage in empirical research in this field are themselves married women who work and are, therefore, emotionally involved in the

71

subject matter. Even they may mistake a rationalisation of what they feel to be a 'good' way of life, for logical deduction or logical inference from facts. Bearing in mind this possible source of bias, findings seem to show that the consequences for the woman herself of work outside the home are on the whole beneficial. There seems little doubt that many enjoy the stimulus of an outside occupation. Investigators do not appear to find evidence of undue strain, mental or physical, in spite of complaints of fatigue. Stressful effects for the woman appear most likely to arise when there are young children to cope with. Not only are their demands physically exhausting, but their illnesses and the provision for supervising them can be worrying. Indeed, it would appear that one reason for the apparently beneficial effects of outside employment on many married women is that, as many of them, whether full-time or part-time, are over thirty-five, they are not for the most part exposed to the worry and fatigue of caring for very young children. In these circumstances, *role-strain*, that is when the demands of two or more roles conflict, as they do if the wife tries to combine the expressive domestic role of home-maker with the instrumental role of supplementary wage earner in a competitive masculine environment, is likely to be minimal, although it may always be present to some extent.

The home-centred woman

Although the re-entry of married women in early middle age into employment is not yet completely established in the minds of all women as part of their normal expectations, there is evidence in a recent government survey that many women look forward to a career only temporarily disrupted for child-rearing. Many of them have mothers who work so that the pattern is already established in a way it was not a generation ago, and it is a trend which may well accelerate. Meanwhile, for those who are excluded from employment for any reason, opportunities for constructive community activities are probably diminishing as well as less obvious, at a time when some of the more glaring inequalities have been ironed out by state action, than they were a generation or so ago. Many of the 'created' social service activities of today, particularly in the middle class, are at the level of charity cocktail parties or of the dispensing of tea to hospital out-patients, the one a legacy of attitudes of the past, the other 'useful' in a narrow sense, but hardly providing a stimulating outlet for an active mind. Voluntary social service and kindred activities no longer offer the challenges they did in the days when Louisa M. Twining was taking 'sunshine to the Workhouse' or Mrs Pember Reeves was bringing the texture of family life in Lambeth on a pound a week to the attention of her complacent contemporaries, or Florence Night-ingale was suppressing the Mrs Gamps, making nursing respectable and hospitals places in which survival was 'probable rather than possible'.

Squalor, degradation, exploitation and criminality still exist, but those with time to do the old-style voluntary work no longer live within walking and *seeing* distance of their less well-heeled fellow citizens, as did the prosperous Victorian wives. They are now mostly concentrated and isolated, hygienically, in commuter communities, half an hour away by fast car, in areas where there is only a limited call for social work, remote from the needy, the bedridden, the aged poor, the morally depraved and the problem families. Thus we have a partial explanation of why voluntary social work, still an acceptable and status-giving activity, has become for some (though not for all, it must be stressed) a way of enriching their own social lives with a snowballing round of coffee mornings and cocktail parties, rather than an attempt to deal squarely with urgent problems. This, of course, is not to say that money-raising activities are not vital, but merely to underline that a surfeit of this kind of activity is unsatisfying to many educated married women, and one more reason why they may turn to paid employment, when their ages and family circumstances permit.

Disappointingly few married women enter local government, in which there is an evident need for intelligent appraisal of and action in community affairs. Some of women's reluctance to engage in local politics is associated with the demands of family life. Regular com-mittee work in the evenings, for example, if conscientiously pursued, is time-consuming and disruptive of family and social life. Participa-tion in local government also costs money, and women in every social stratum, with few exceptions, are poorer than men of the same level, and there always tend to be immediate, pressing family demands on their more slender purses—unexpected replacements of torn clothing, a few shillings here and there for school outings, Christmas stockings to be filled, the celebration meal for the special occasion, the extras for the sick child and so on.

Limitations on opportunities for satisfying extra-familial activities are perhaps secondary, but they constitute strongly supporting reasons why so many educated married women turn to paid employment to fulfil the urge to use their talents. An acute shortage of womanpower in jobs requiring qualifications and a good level of ability has given impetus to the drift to work. One investigation shows shortages of professional woman-power of quite startling proportions.[6] It would appear that the wastage of professional skill among women is not great; that those not working at all are either retired or are housebound by the presence of young children. Many of them express the wish to return to their work, especially where the rewards are relatively large as in medicine. Of the better-educated women who wish to work after marriage about two-thirds become involved with teaching in some form. Among the reasons here are the obvious: career opportunities in a profession with much-publicised shortages,[7] and hours and holidays minimally disruptive of family life.

It is sometimes argued that married women of every educational and social stratum have an obligation to work outside the home, except for a few years when engaged actively in child-rearing. Myrdal and Klein[8] ably summarise the main considerations usually advanced from this point of view. They are: that the economy cannot afford to support active able-bodied women in unproductive roles; that to have borne and reared a small family is too easy a passport to idleness after 40; that it is unfair to men, and immoral for women to live as parasites on the efforts of others; that it is better for the woman herself who will (a) by-pass the neuroses of middle age, (b) insure herself against being cast aside by the father of her children in favour of someone younger and more sexually attractive, (c) find a sense of purpose in life, (d) make herself a more interesting person.

Arguments such as these are usually put forward most strenuously by educated dedicated career women leading full and interesting lives themselves. Other points of view are equally arguable. As we have seen, jobs which suit a woman's abilities and which will not disrupt domestic life are not always readily available, and in any case with the fashion for larger families (evident until 1965 but recently halted again) the period of active motherhood may well soon extend further into middle life for many. Men do not usually complain. To support their wives is part of their expectations at present, and far from thinking of their wives as parasites, many enjoy the protective and authoritative role which accrues to the office of breadwinner, not much of a justification perhaps in the eyes of some feminists, but a fact of society as it is. Many also sincerely believe that wives at home contribute indirectly to the economy by increasing male productivity. And it can certainly be less immoral simply to sit at home all day than to engage in some sorts of gainful employment, such as prostitution to give an extreme example, or even perhaps certain sorts of sales promotion. In respect of the third type of argument there is no universal recipe for avoiding neurosis in middle age, or at any other age, if physical, emotional and environmental factors are all interacting in complicated ways; a job may or may not be helpful in individual cases. As for insurance against desertion in middle life, to stay at home and keep the male heart tenderly beating by cherishing the adjacent stomach in the old-fashioned way, might even be as good a bet.

There are other ways of achieving a sense of purpose without working for money, and no one way is right for all women. Most of those faced with empty years after 40 solve their own dilemma without becoming neurotic malcontents. Some take up cultural activities (these are the women labelled by the intellectual snobs as 'the culture vultures') and find these enrich their lives and enliven their conversation; Etruscan art is as good a conversational gambit as what the boss said. Many middle-aged women find an outlet in an expansion of domestic activities; housekeeping, as Parkinson might have it, expands to fill the time available. Roundly condemned by some feminists, the homemade bread, the rhubarb wine, the continental cookery, the self-conscious flower arrangements are creative activities and, for

75

women of the right temperament, more satisfying than some routine job in office or factory. For women of a different temperament there are still opportunities for voluntary service to the community for those who seek them and which provide satisfying outlets for some. Many more could probably use their middle years usefully if the goodwill which appears to exist in the suburbs were channelled into constructive activities such as community organisation, and if some of the disincentives were removed from local politics.

Socialisation

Socialisation is the process of preparing the individual to respond appropriately to the demands of his society. It is a learning process which can go on throughout life, so there is no rigid demarcation between socialisation and education. Both perform a training function for society which contributes to its continuity and stability in so far as each rising generation is prepared in readiness to take on the social roles and positions of the preceding generations. From the perspective of the individual, both play a part in fitting him for the roles and positions to which he will succeed by making available to him the knowledge and skills he will need, by transmitting the rules by which he will be expected to direct his activities, by tailoring his personality so that he can adjust adequately to the requirements of his culture, and by providing a setting within which he can develop reason, self-control, conscience and attitudes of co-operation, all of which are necessary for social life.

The *primary* socialisation from infancy through the early years of childhood normally takes place within a family setting except in the cases of those who are for some reason deprived of parental care. At this stage the foundations of personality are laid, basic physical skills such as perception and muscular co-ordination are acquired, and the rudiments of reasoning ability become evident. Most authorities agree that the early childhood years are crucial for learning to integrate effectively in social situations. The type of socialisation a child receives, and hence his chances in life, are thus greatly dependent on the type of family into which he is born, on the aspects of the culture which are transmitted to him, and the means by which this is done. Mental, physical, moral and emotional development may all be retarded in the absence of suitable social stimuli; and poverty, infection, emotional insecurity and substandard parental example are all cultural hindrances to satisfactory socialisation. Poor heredity is also an impediment; and conversely, a favourable environment maximises the chance that inherited physique and intelligence will realise their full potential.

Certain needs are common to all young children if growth and personality development are to take place in a favourable environment. Among the most obvious are a family income sufficient to provide proper nourishment, decent housing with good sanitation and sleeping arrangements appropriate to age and sex, fresh air, adequate clothing and space to play both indoors and out. There should be plenty to do, plenty of action and things happening at home, and other children to play with. There should be helpful adults who encourage intelligent questions and answer them sensibly, and who will give guidance in developing skills such as walking, talking and manual dexterity, in solving problems of how to fulfil the expectations of others, in learning how to use initiative and how to avoid danger and to cope with frustrations. And if there can also be interesting conversation, educated friends, books available and help in making use of them, so much the better.

Differences in development occur between town and country; the rural child may be healthier as a result of fresh food and fresh air, the urban child may develop sharper wits. Factors such as the religion and the racial origin of parents have an effect; members of 'out-groups' tend to develop recognisable character traits. Social class is important and shows up in speech, in attitudes to thrift and spending, in friendliness or aggression, in education, in aspirations, and in methods of child-rearing. The location of the home is important as a partial determinant of values and goals. Children too from an early age will vary greatly in their experiences of life. Some will lead narrow circumscribed lives. Confinement in a detached villa in a large garden can be almost as isolating as confinement in a top-storey local authority flat. Some, in all social classes, will lead lives packed with activity and interests. The child living in a crowded street, himself a part of a large kinship network, absorbing the conversation of his aunts and uncles on the concrete facts of life, be it on obstetrical ordeals, industrial disputes or greyhound racing, who is permitted to wander freely and taste the heady excitements of city streets and shops, may well have a highly stimulating environment if he survives the obvious hazards such as traffic and 'bad company'. The child insulated in a 'desirable residence' may well be better nourished and breathe purer air than his working-class counterpart. He is likely to be protected from physical danger and sheltered from conversations recounting the more gruesome and gruelling details of birth, life and death. He may have parents who are highly educated but who nevertheless may well not be adequately tuned in to the interests of the young, and he may hear little adult conversation except in terms of abstractions he is not yet equipped to comprehend. Furthermore, playing on an expensive climbing frame, in however elegant a garden, does not necessarily provide exercise, test courage or challenge the spirit of adventure any better than jumping on and off a moving bus to the accompanying invective of the conductor. To be born into a high socioeconomic stratum does not guarantee a propitious child-rearing milieu although, other things being equal, middle- and upper-class children have advantages, the suburb has the edge over the slum, Hampstead over Stepney.

It is necessary to distinguish between the process of socialisation and the psychological aspects of the developmental process. Clearly the two interact, but it is not our purpose to enlarge upon the psychological aspects. Our concern is with the inter-relationships of family, external environment and personality. However, theories of socialisation, in this sense, use psychological as well as sociological concepts. Those from psychology relate mainly to learning theory.

The degree, type and quality of family interaction influence the way in which a child's personality develops. Imitation is known to be an important part of learning, and the child becomes aware of and copies actions and attitudes he sees around him, and internalises them. Many types of behaviour such as a way of speaking or certain mannerisms are learned, and ways of behaving, formerly thought to be innate, such as aggression, or sloth, can be shown to be learned. The child's earliest observations are of his own most intimate social group, usually the family into which he was born, and its members provide the principal models with which he can identify as well as imitate. The models his family members can provide are limited by their own cultural environment, so that whatever are the social or other limitations of his family of origin, these become part of his personality too. Even when he does not actually imitate, he does not remain unaffected, for his environment, which includes as an important component the behaviour of parents and other family members, defines the limits within which he *can* learn or act.

'Behaviour' means not only the ways in which actions are performed, such as table manners, but also a whole set of attitudes, motivations and role expectations which are also learned by imitation. People are seen to behave in particular ways, so that the child comes to realise that people interact in accordance with certain expectations. For example, when he is ill, his mother responds in one way, the doctor in another. He also perceives that the acceptable limits within which roles are performed are set by the sanctions of society. For example, a father, as the principal breadwinner in the family, may be expected to provide a sufficient income but not, in our society, by dishonest or violent means. He is subject to social control. His own socialisation will have provided him with reference points to guide him in distinguishing between acceptable and unacceptable methods of acquisition, both within his own sub-culture and within the culture of the larger society.

Most children, similarly, learn to conform to what their own environments demand, and those who deviate appreciably from this standard are regarded as abnormal. The greater the coincidence between familial and societal norms, the less will be the personal stress involved in internalising appropriate modes of behaviour. If family norms deviate seriously from the more general societal norms, for example with regard to respect for property, then the child sooner or later becomes aware of two sets of conflicting norms that he must try to reconcile, norms which include values, attitudes, beliefs and patterns of behaviour. This is a formidable task for a young child, and the conflicts which arise have been shown to be inimical to the development of personality. The more stable the society, the more 'traditional' the family structure, the less will be the personal stress involved in making behavioural choices.

Given a situation where the child's material needs are adequately met, the children who thrive best are likely to be those who receive consistent parental love, encouragement and discipline. Erratic handling causes anxiety and insecurity. Material deprivation and emotional insecurity in combination are known to correlate with various kinds of social deviance, including delinquency. Maladjustment, too, is highly correlated with unsatisfactory homes and is manifested in symptoms such as withdrawal, retardation and aggression. Children showing such symptoms are frequently the products of homes where the parents quarrel, where he is used as a weapon in parental fights, and also where the parents are incessantly preoccupied with their own concerns or careers. A child is also at a disadvantage when he is a member of a real 'problem' family, that is one seriously deficient in its ability to organize its own affairs. In all such home situations children become anxious and insecure, their personalities tend to be stunted, and they are seriously handicapped in the acquisition of acceptable standards of behaviour.

Favourable conditions for personality development must include the opportunity to make warm emotional relationships with parents or parent substitutes, if the child is to develop normal social responsiveness. Some authorities regard the first three years as crucial, so it follows that the quality and quantity of maternal care is vital. The importance of the emotional aspects of mothering has been underlined by the work of John Bowlby who drew attention to the stunting effects of maternal deprivation. His thesis is that the separation of a young child from its mother, or reliable mother substitute, for any length of time, affects negatively his personality structure and hence his future prospects. As a consequence of 'maternal deprivation' Bowlby identified what he called the 'affectionless' personality, unloving and unlovable, afraid to give or receive affection. He was further able to demonstrate that among those involved in certain areas of disturbed or deviant behaviour there was a high proportion of 'affectionless' personalities who had been deprived of maternal care.

Anthropologists such as Margaret Mead have been quick to point out that there are many successful patterns of child-rearing which are different from our own. In some societies the institutions inhibit close, permanent ties with either parent, as for instance when breast-feeding and genuine responsibility for the care of the child is shared among a number of women. However, such arrangements do not necessarily mean that the child is deprived of *personal* care and of the feelings of satisfaction and security it gives, particularly when, as in primitive societies, the diffusion of child care responsibilities is within a kingroup. One of the conclusions on the relation between culture and personality which may be tentatively drawn from anthropological evidence of this kind would seem to be that child-rearing practices must be culturally appropriate; it does nothing to disprove the idea that in our own society the personal care of a mother figure *is* the most appropriate way to provide the emotional satisfactions necessary in the early years.

In a large survey [1] of nearly 5000 L.C.C. legitimate children under five years old 52 per cent were found to have suffered some separation from their mother. It would seem, therefore, that it is a not uncommon occurrence. But not all separations are long ones nor are they necessarily associated with other distressing events, and it was found that the effect of the 'maternal deprivation' depended upon the circumstances. The children in this sample who showed the fewest signs of distress (e.g. nightmares, thumb-sucking) were those who remained in their own homes for the period of the separation. It could be argued from this that children form attachments to particular places as well as to particular people. Nevertheless, the evidence supports Bowlby's thesis to the extent that long separations from the mother were associated with disturbances in the child. The findings of other studies, too, although only partially substantiating Bowlby's work, suggest that a modification rather than an abandonment of his theory is called for. Evidence from a large all-class survey in Newcastle [2] (1142 babies) underlines the importance of the quality of mothering in the mental as well as the physical health of the child. Hilda Lewis and Harriet Wilson have similarly laid stress on the quality of maternal care. Later workers, in fact, far from exploding Bowlby's theory have refined it by drawing attention to the existence of *partial* maternal deprivation. Even when the mother is physically present, her child is deprived if she performs her role indifferently by failing to foster a warm, loving and secure relationship with a high degree of consistency and continuity.

The satisfaction of the child's emotional needs by the mother or an adequate substitute is only one of the elements in the formation of personality. Its actual importance in a particular case depends on a number of variables such as age at deprivation, his previous experience of affection, various environmental factors including school, neighbourhood and friendships, genetic factors such as intelligence, and even on factors such as malnutrition, it has been suggested. The weighting of the other variables would account for the differing effects of maternal deprivation in so far as some children manifest severe disturbance and others are apparently unharmed. Because of the difficulties in identifying the variables involved and in assessing their relative importance, knowledge in this field has no great precision and propositions about the effects of maternal deprivation on personality formation and social behaviour generally must be treated with caution and modified when necessary in the light of new knowledge. Nevertheless the implications of Bowlby's work for communities such as our own where mothers increasingly work outside the home are of importance, even although it has not yet been proven either that the 'affectionless' personality cannot be changed by more felicitous experiences later in life, or that it stands in a causal relationship to all the kinds of deviant behaviour with which it has been associated.

A by-product of the great interest in maternal deprivation has been a tendency to overlook the crucial role of the father in the socialisation process. It can, of course, be argued that inadequate father–child and husband–wife relationships form part of the complex of variables that produce the inadequate mother–child relationship which itself constitutes partial maternal deprivation. But 'paternal deprivation' appears to be a reality in its own right, so to speak, and it would seem to have as great a claim to a place in the aetiology of deviant behaviour as the maternal variety. One study has shown that many more delinquent than non-delinquent boys felt themselves to be 'father-rejected'.[3]

It seems that the delinquent boys felt that their mothers loved them more than their fathers, whereas non-delinquents tended to feel loved equally by both parents. The delinquents, too, were more afraid of their fathers than of their mothers, whereas the non-delinquents often chose to go to their fathers when they were in difficulties. The *rapport* between father and delinquent son was poor, and the authority of the father less than in the eyes of non-delinquent sons.

It can be inferred from this and other evidence that when fathers play their roles defectively or reject their children, the personality development of the child will be affected. *Both* parents are important. However, we must again beware of drawing facile conclusions. In the case of delinquency, for example, there seems little doubt that many delinquents have poor relationships with one or both parents; but in some cases the poor relationships might well be a result rather than a cause of the delinquencies. Because both parents have a role to play in the personality development of the child, it would seem too that he is at a disadvantage if he is a member of an incomplete family, with one parent frequently or completely absent as in situations either when the father or mother is dead, when there has been separation or divorce, or when the mother is unmarried. Attention has recently been drawn to the plight of fatherless families, who whatever the reason for the father's absence are likely to suffer not only emotional deprivation, but material deprivation as well. Many are in severe financial need and mothers go out to work for this reason so aggravating the emotional difficulties in alleviating the material ones.

Although the figures available are not very precise, it would appear that there has recently been a considerable increase in the number of mothers of all kinds who have children under school age and who leave them with minders while they themselves go out to work. Ignoring, for the moment, the much-publicised and appalling 'arrangements' which are made for the care of some of the children involved, the implications for the personality development even of those for whom good care is arranged may be far reaching. Care in day nurseries or with competent and conscientious minders cannot but be less close and personal than that of a good mother. Such evidence as we have on impersonal methods of child-rearing is not encouraging.

Leaving out of account the studies which have been made on institutionalised children in our own country, who are not a 'normal' sample in the sense that they are often from deprived backgrounds, it is said that on the Kibbutzim of Israel, where contact with the natural parents is highly regulated and children are socialised mainly within the peer group under the supervision of experts, the adults who emerge show a very long dependence on the peer group. Maturity requires emancipation from the control of peers as well as from that of parents. Adult dependency on either amounts to the prolongation of attitudes appropriate to childhood or adolescence.

Methods of child care

We have indicated that the personality structure of the child is influenced by the way in which the parents discharge their fundamental tasks of nurture and control. In the performance of these functions parents in modern societies usually carry more personal responsibility than they do in traditional societies. Not only do they often lack the support of a kinship network in close proximity, but there are more choices open to them. Manuals of child care proffer advice and recommend régimes which are not only alternatives, but sometimes contradictory ones at that. Traditional practices have lost their sanctity as fashions come and go. Societal norms are fluid and parental roles, along with other roles in society, have become indistinct and the conflicting cultural expectations which arise in these circumstances are matched by ambivalent parental attitudes towards the child. It seems to be more than ever difficult, notwithstanding the new psychological and other knowledge, to be sure that the methods of child care adopted will achieve the goal of acceptable and responsible adult behaviour, particularly as different adult milieux demand different attitudes and values.

Certain child-rearing practices are thought to be associated with particular personality structures in later life, although not all the experts agree on the real effects of the methods adopted. In so far as there are differences in opinion or in the interpretation of evidence, many of them centre around restrictions placed on the child. Early

85

and strict discipline is thought by some writers to promote a strong conscience useful in maintaining social order. The most notable of the modern exponents of discipline was a New Zealander, Dr (later Sir) Truby King, whose work has exerted great influence throughout the English-speaking world and beyond for thirty or more years. The disciplined and Spartan régime he recommended (initially drawn from his experiments in raising calves!) was dominated by the clock. 'His (the baby's) education begins in the first week,' we are told, 'good habits being established which remain all his life.'[4] Strict mealtimes must be observed with nothing but boiled water or fruit juice between them. No night feeds are allowed; if he does not settle 'give him an ounce or so of boiled water—no milk'.[5] 'Beware of the spoilt cry.' 'If you know that baby (is loved, well cared for and not ill) leave him to cry it out! Don't give in, or he will be master of the house—not you!'[6] A healthy baby in his second year may have a cold bath each morning, a practice also urged upon mothers losing their milk. Addressed to mothers in every part of the British Empire, it was admirably designed, whether intentionally or not, to turn out the personality type fitted to build, defend and govern an Empire, or to be suitable wives to those who did; that is people with determination, fortitude, self-control, not afraid of physical hardship, yet well nourished and cared for and so able to withstand infection. For the middle- and upper-class Englishman the process begun in a Truby King nursery was later consolidated by an old-style public school education with its emphasis on courage, loyalty, honour and service to the community. Not that the Truby King régime was exclusive to any one social class. In so far as it was used in hospitals and recommended in clinics, it permeated all social levels.

Many authorities at present deplore severe discipline, maintaining that it leads to personality disorders, particularly those associated with over-anxiety, and pointing out that an over-developed conscience can lead to crippling feelings of guilt. Chief among those who have popularised this viewpoint with mothers is Dr Benjamin Spock. The tone of his best-selling baby book[7] is set by its first sentence, 'You know more than you think you do', and the explanation of this statement is summed up two paragraphs later in the words '. . . what good mothers and fathers instinctively feel like doing for their babies is best after all'. And this goes for each stage of development. It is up to the parents to provide the means for physical, emotional and intellectual growth and allow the child to enter each stage when he is ready for it, not *before* but at the proper time in accordance with *their* child's needs. 'You can't hurry him' is another key phrase in this flexible and permissive régime. 'Strict' training will only make the baby rebellious. Sooner or later he will conform to the expected pattern without pushing. He will develop good manners, amiability and so on if he has sensible parents who themselves behave well, says Dr Spock. He will develop self-confidence too, if he is accepted and appreciated for what he is, and not always being measured against some standard the parents would like to see him attain. Dr Spock has recently clarified his position by stating that he does not see himself as the instigator of permissiveness, which he regards as a trend gaining momentum for most of this century. Although we cannot ignore the full implications of the phrase 'Your baby knows best', Dr Spock now declares himself in favour of some firmness in dealing with children. He supports clear parental leadership in laying down standards and in expecting conformity to them. Firm leadership, he tells us, aids the child in his search for identity. But with no clear guide from Dr Spock or others as to the degree of restriction which is necessary if the child is ultimately to conform to adult standards of behaviour, and which at the same time he can tolerate without imposing undue stresses upon him, it is not surprising to find that actual practices vary on a continuum from the extremely permissive to the harshly punitive and demanding. There are innumerable combinations and permutations of rewards and punishments.

The effects of punishment are by no means constant. It seems that the attitudes of the parents, and particularly of the mother, are important, whether they are 'accepting', that is, allowing the child to behave in ways appropriate to childhood rather than expecting him to be a miniature adult, or whether they are 'rejecting'. Discipline, including punishment, when imposed by a warm, accepting parent has positive effects, it appears, for the child's development. But when a cold, rejecting parent punishes, the effects are unlikely to be what was

87

intended, even when no element of harshness is involved. Indeed the importance of a warm, loving parent–child relationship would appear to be paramount for the development of the child and it should be kept in mind that there are parents who are in varying degrees warm-accepting and cold-rejecting in all social groups.

Although a growing permissiveness has been a *general* trend in most areas of child care, *actual* practices vary. There are differences between geographical areas, between town and country, between races and between social classes. The intelligence, educational level and the personality structure of the mother are also relevant to differences in child-rearing.[8] In a small country such as our own, regional practices vary less than in the continent of Europe where traditional peasant communities are still widespread, or than in the vast expanses of America. Children in areas which are remote and pastoral, where certain commercial products for baby care are not easily available, and where values tend to be conservative, will be brought up differently from children living in a metropolis where fashions and cosmopolitan values permeate readily. In our own country there are broad differences between the North with its evangelical tradition, economically dependent largely on arduous work in heavy industries, and the South with its variety of light, clean jobs in industry and commerce; for the parents have, or acquire, different attitudes and are socialising their children for different life chances. Regional differences would seem to be closely bound up in particular with occupational differences, and with religious tradition as a strong secondary influence. Race is also important, particularly when ethnic factors result in exclusion from the larger society. In addition sex, age, position in the family, the presence or absence of one or both parents and the parental ages all affect the way a child will experience the socialisation process. All in all it is very difficult indeed to disentangle and give due weight to the various influences at work.

Of all the variables, the personality structure of mother appears to be of central importance. A mother chooses certain training methods and provides a certain social environment partly because of her own personality, itself in part the product of her own early experiences in her family of origin. Her actual practices will be affected, too, by the social pressures which may be on her at the time, and any family tensions she may be experiencing can be significant. It has been shown, for example, that the quality of the marital relationship, that is the degree of adjustment between the husband and wife, and also the wife's satisfaction with the husband's performance of his role, affect the degree of warmth experienced by the children. It seems that unsatisfactory marital relationships are correlated with unsatisfactory parent–child relationships. It does not appear, as might be assumed, that a coldness in the marriage is compensated by extra warmth towards the children.[9]

Of the other possible variables, certain demographic factors may be important. The mother's age has significance. If she is young, she may have energy, and she will be young with her children; she may also be flighty, unready to take on the mature responsibilities of motherhood; her income may be low, and her housing unsuitable, if her husband is young also. If she is older, there are less likely to be pressing financial difficulties; she will have had time to make up her mind what she wants from life and she will have a variety of experience on which to draw to help her make decisions; but she may be very far removed from her child by the gap in years, and she may tire easily, although many older mothers have been shown to have more stamina, when they are in good health.

The number of her children is an influence. If there are too many too close she may simply be grossly overworked and unable to give to each the attention it needs. Not all children in a family experience the same degree of care. Evidence from a number of studies suggests that in general an eldest or only child receives much care because his mother has time to give and is anxious to achieve perfection, and that the youngest receives much warmth. By inference this means that the children in between, a sizeable proportion of the total child population, are to some extent 'left out'. It must not be assumed that this is always so; nevertheless size of family and order of birth have an effect on socialisation in so far as they affect the mother's handling of her child.

The child's sex also makes a difference. In general children are reared in such a way that they are from an early age able to identify themselves with their own sex, and the way in which they are treated throughout childhood serves to consolidate their sex identification, although in some ways less distinction is made than two or three decades ago. Nevertheless, however many toys are shared, boys and girls are still given toys which are in some ways associated with adult masculine and feminine activities, toy trains and dolls being the classic examples. That a boy will make his way in the world and that a girl will marry and thus provide herself with full board and lodging (in spite of the evidence that many women now want to work outside the home and wish they had some training) is still the apparent expectation underlying many of the attitudes parents adopt towards their children; they often feel that education is more important for a boy; they are often more tolerant of aggression in boys and more likely to encourage them to 'hit back'. A boy is also more likely to receive corporal punishment, a fact not wholly connected only with his seemingly greater propensity for misdemeanour, but as part of a toughening process to acclimatise him to taking 'knocks' in a ruthless adult society.

Of the other socialisation variables, much the most attention has been paid to social class. Positive attitudes towards parenthood are stronger in some strata than in others.

It is clear that a child's social class determines some, although not all, of the important formative influences to which he is exposed. Most of the studies on this topic generalise in terms of the 'working class' and the 'middle class', as if there were only two classes. Clearly this is an over-simplification. Not only is there a small upper class [1] which is either resistant to or neglected by sociologists in their empirical investigations, but every 'class' contains a number of substrata each of which has its own characteristics which distinguish it from the others. The classes and the substrata within them also overlap in various ways; for example a working-class occupation, working-class values and a middle-class income might be found in combination. The people within the broad class groupings also create divisions in their own minds which have reality for the understanding of social phenomena, for example the 'respectable' and the 'rough' working class. Every 'class', too, contains a range of occupations, incomes, intelligence, educational levels, religious beliefs and ethical norms. All this must be borne in mind, together with other variables we have already identified as important in the socialisation process, and which are the monopoly of no particular social stratum, such as the degree of harmony in the marital relationship. Provided we are aware of these limitations, it is possible to make certain broad generalisations which help us to understand the effect of social class on the socialisation process in so far as early childhood experiences and specific training techniques can be said to produce recognisable personality traits. As class practices have oscillated during the present century it is very difficult to show that this is the case; but the values underlying the practices may well have altered much less than the practices themselves, and they too form part of early experience.

Feeding habits have been extensively studied and form a good example of the transience of class stereotypes. Traditionally, working-class women breast-fed their babies for long periods; they also fed them irregularly on demand. Middle-class women had other means available. The 1912 edition of Mrs Beeton's *Household Management*, which was addressed to the middle classes, contained a long section on selecting and supervising the wet nurse. Its inclusion in a book intended to be generally helpful and authoritative on domestic matters suggests that, even in this century, the employment of wet nurses was not so uncommon as might be supposed. Bottle-feeding became popular with the middle classes as its safety increased. This was partly a matter of fashion; the fashionable women (the former employers of wet nurses) adopted bottle-feeding. Indeed, bottle-feeding itself became one of the indicators of social class and so was adopted by the socially aspiring, who in any case like to be regarded as fastidious. It was easy to rationalise as in keeping with a scientific age for the quality and quantity of milk could be controlled. It was also a great convenience for the pleasure-loving and to a few of the new career women, who could go their ways confident that they were doing their scientific best for their babies, and freed from the nagging anxiety that a wet nurse would secretly indulge a taste for gin and pickles in preference to tapioca pudding.

The working-class woman was largely debarred from participating in 'scientific' baby care, not only as a consequence of the prejudices of the inadequately educated, but also, in a period of recurrent trade depression, by the cost. Not infrequently, she lacked elementary amenities in the kitchen, so that breast-feeding was often not only cheaper but actually more convenient for her, and it was also encouraged by health visitors and others as cleaner and safer for the baby. As working-class real incomes, housing and education improved, and with the availability of subsidised dried milk, bottle-feeding in the working class has become the preferred method. Contrariwise, breast-feeding is currently highly esteemed in the middle class; so is feeding on demand. Bottles and rigid schedules are out, the breast on demand is in. Science, this time psychoanalytically oriented, has decreed that mothers' milk as supplied from prehistoric times onwards is best after all. The middle-class mothers, more literate, with quicker access to the newest ideas have abandoned their predilection for the bottle, for mothers in general are strongly motivated to do their best for their children. In some cases they may also be capitalising the current status-giving properties of the breast, for conformity to fashion is also a powerful persuader.

It would appear that many working-class mothers are ignoring the exhortations of clinic staffs to revert to breast-feeding.[2] The reasons for this reluctance are not entirely clear. Their houses still often lack privacy compared with those of middle-class mothers, and a larger proportion go out to work and want to get back as soon as possible, although the Newsons did not consider this class difference great enough to account for the difference in the incidence of breast-feeding. It has been suggested too that for many the feeding bottle symbolises their own emancipation from the extreme privation and interminable drudgery of their mothers' generation. It could even be that the cult of the concave bosom is reinforcing the bottle preference among the very young mothers, a group which is predominantly of the working class. The influences at work have not yet been sufficiently carefully identified and analysed for us to be able to assign any relative weights to them.

In some ways, such as being given a dummy or going to bed late, the working-class child is more indulged in the early years than the middle-class child. But he is also more familiar with violence, is more likely to receive corporal punishment, and less likely to know what he is being chastised *for*. The middle-class parent often displays more self-control, and often takes trouble to think out imaginative punishments in Gilbert and Sullivan manner 'to fit the crime'. Working-class discipline is more likely to be erratic, to vacillate between over-indulgence and maiming violence, but even when such extremes are not evident, discipline has been shown to be more frequently inconsistent than in middle-class families. Middle-class punishment, too, of whatever kind often takes into account the intention of the wrongdoer, for example whether a breakage was deliberate or accidental, whereas the tendency in the working class is to punish for the act itself, or its consequences. On all these matters the evidence in

93

relation to class differences is remarkably consistent for both Britain and the United States.

One way and another the myth of working-class warmth and permissiveness has now been largely exploded. Life is harsher on the whole than for the middle-class child, and attitudes are more authoritarian, although it should be remembered that at all levels there will be a sprinkling of parents who are punitive, repressive and unimaginative in their attitudes towards their children. There is more discussion of disciplinary techniques among middle-class parents, indeed a greater verbal facility enables them to communicate more readily with one another and with their children. It is thus possible to reason with the child, and verbalisation of itself can help to resolve tensions without resort to action. An impoverished vocabulary, scant in the adjectives and adverbs necessary to convey shades of meaning and describe emotions, impairs communication for many working-class parents, hence they are apt to resort more precipitately to shouting and smacking.

The verbal skill of middle-class parents and their children not only allows them to discuss situations and feelings, it also enables the favoured middle-class disciplinary techniques to be used effectively. Middle-class techniques of control have been called 'love oriented', which means that a direct or indirect threat of the withdrawal of love is made. Thus, praise, attitudes of approval or disappointment and so on, are purposively communicated to the child as sanctions, and isolation is used as a punishment with its implied or threatened withdrawal of love. The authoritarian injunctions of the working class are translated into terms of emotional blackmail. It is said that these 'love oriented' methods of discipline are guilt-producing, that they result in a strict conscience, which in the end leads the child to discipline itself, irrespective of the presence of an authority figure be it parent, teacher or policeman. It is further argued that they give him an awareness of the feelings of others, the capacity to face up to difficulties and to cope with them, and an ability to take a long-term view of his behaviour in relation to future events and prospects. It must, however, be remembered here that in the middle class he is also backed by the resources which enable him to harness his endeavours to long-term objectives.

The working class on the other hand has been said to live on the 'pleasure principle'; if satisfactions are within reach they are taken at once. This immediacy reflects and is reflected in disciplinary practices. The effects of the usual type of punishment, that is corporal, frequently unpremeditated, or the withdrawal of privileges, are immediately felt. They are also in essence retributive, so that the child feels free to repeat the same misdemeanour so long as he is prepared to pay the price. They give him little idea of what *is* expected of him unless they are accompanied by a consistent parental example of 'good' behaviour. In these circumstances conscience remains rudimentary, and the motivation, if any, to behave is fear. Thus, although working-class discipline appears strict, it is less effective in the long run than the love-oriented, guilt-producing techniques. As with punishment, working-class rewards are also direct and tangible; sweets and treats, rather than approval.

It is important not to over-emphasise techniques as such as has sometimes been done in the past, for techniques are the external stimuli applied to encourage or reinforce the desired behaviour. The newer approach is to focus attention on the total early environment including its emotional climate, values and goals. The life chances, and the goals and their underlying values, differ by social stratum. They influence and are reflected in the differing socialisation régimes, régimes which operate so that appropriate values become internalised, for the ends of socialisation are seen from divergent perspectives. Both groups want their children to behave well, but the emphasis is on different aspects. The middle class place great value on self-control and honesty, for a high degree of personal integrity is essential in many middle-class occupations such as accountancy and the law. Self-control is also linked with self-denial and thrift, with the postponing of present pleasures for future good or gain, epitomised by the years of effort needed to acquire the qualifications for entry into the professions or to save the capital to start or enlarge a business. A degree of compassion and selflessness is also highly desirable in some middle-class professions such as medicine, nursing and teaching. As the middle-class child is more likely to be taken to church than the working-class child, he is also more likely to hear all these virtues extolled. The middle-class passion for keeping pets, an activity largely denied to those who live in congested, gardenless streets, also serves to awaken feelings of compassion; in the better-off suburbs it seems not unknown for single households with young children periodically to be caring for between ten or twelve pets when the ponies, dogs, cats, rabbits, guinea-pigs, hamsters and their progeny are totted up. In addition boys are expected to be adventurous and brave, qualities which were important middle-class attributes in the recent empire-building past.

An important working-class objective is that the family should be regarded as 'respectable'. Great stress is laid on the child's cleanliness, tidiness and punctuality, and also on obedience, all to the end that he will not discredit the family and will keep out of trouble. The emphasis on obedience is also said to reflect the subservient adult roles that many will be called upon to play later, in the community and at work.

The class distinctions we have been making are in reality stereotypes; the 'working class' and the 'middle class' are far from being two homogeneous groupings. At a time when 'middle-class' aspirations and some would say, attitudes, are permeating the working class, the behaviour and personality types we have designated 'working class' have now probably general applicability at the lower end of the socio-economic scale only. Similarly, some of the behaviour we have called 'middle class', is probably applicable only to some of the upper middle class, to some of those engaged in professional and entrepreneurial-type occupations. Certainly there is much overlapping in the life-styles of the lower middle and upper working classes, though not all sociologists agree that there have been fundamental changes in working-class attitudes since the adoption of bourgeois trappings.[3] There is no doubt, too, that many middle-class occupations demand 'working-class' values and attitudes; for example, a thrusting aggressiveness facilitates success in many middle-class jobs. For these reasons it is suggested that class has been overestimated and occupation underestimated in the importance of their bearing on family behaviour, although as occupation is usually regarded as one of the determinants of class, it is clearly difficult to isolate the influences attributable to occupation alone. However, a number of authorities with social-psychological interests have attempted to do just this, and their findings are of interest, in so far as they constitute some degree of explanation of the differences between and within social strata.

It is hypothesised that the way the family links with the economy determines child-rearing practices, or is an important influence on them. With regard to discipline, for example, it has been shown that at most middle-class levels, and certainly at the high-income ones, a mother and father behave with about equal severity or leniency as the case may be towards their children. As the social scale is descended, the father becomes progressively more severe than the mother in the punishment of the children. Some writers have explained this as a function of the father's inadequacy or frustration in his job. He is said to compensate for his lack of prestige at work by his authoritarianism at home. In general, if an individual craves power or feels prestige to be his due, if his job is boring, lacks opportunities and provides inadequate scope for his abilities, his frustration is likely to become manifest in authoritarian attitudes, it is argued. An outcome of such attitudes may be to throw mother and child into a closer relationship than might otherwise have happened. The evidence for this supposition is not altogether consistent, but those who support this viewpoint also hypothesise that a close mother–son relationship predisposes boys to over-identify with their mothers, and inhibits them from standing on their own feet in difficulties or crises, and as a consequence from filling responsible jobs with credit in later life. The middle-class father, on the other hand, whose behaviour at home is authoritative rather than authoritarian, is much more likely to have a satisfying job which stretches his abilities and enables him to exercise power by virtue of which he is accorded prestige. For these reasons, it is argued, he is more likely to behave with restraint at home and to be more receptive to the satisfactions of family life. This line of argument, that those who achieve job satisfaction are less prone to pursue authoritarian behaviour in the family, can also be used to explain differing degrees of harshness within the same class or social grouping; it helps to explain why some middle-class fathers are authoritarian and some working-class fathers are not. The explanation lies in the degree of job satisfaction he experiences rather than in his social class.

Family links with the economy may also provide a partial explanation of the growth of middle-class permissiveness in child-rearing. Some occupations such as those in the professions, those of an entrepreneurial type, and the one-man business, to give a few examples, still call for the traditional middle-class qualities of self-control, initiative, competitive independence, decision-making and calculated risk-taking. Other middle-class jobs increasingly require conformity and the ability to fit easily into a hierarchy of authority, and these qualities are particularly in demand for jobs which form part of a bureaucratic structure within which the limits of individual authority are strictly defined and decisions are formalised through specific channels. Large-scale manufacture or the civil service, for example, are bureaucratic organisations requiring people who will respect the norms and ethos of the organisation. Self-control and ambition, in particular, remain important, but other traditional middle-class values and personal qualities have largely given way to those conducive to 'getting on' in an organisation, such as being well liked and maintaining a general appearance of *bonhomie*. It follows that the personality characteristics most highly rewarded in a bureaucratic structure are those fostered by permissive, loving and friendly parental care.[4]

Secondary socialisation

The family is the most important agency of primary socialisation, but as the child grows older he is exposed to a wider variety of social contacts, and agencies other than the family play an increasingly important part in the *secondary* socialisation process which follows. Sooner or later he will find that the norms of other groups differ from those of his family, and so he discovers new points of reference, develops new loyalties, and is often strongly motivated to conform to these extra-familial group norms particularly when non-conformity might have unpleasant consequences.

Some of the child's most formative experiences are likely to derive from his school, which in the earlier years usually is itself part of his home neighbourhood. In modern Britain the school is regarded as the most important of the secondary socialising agencies. In the textbooks of a generation ago it was usually assumed that family educational functions had been eroded to a state little more than vestigial. Although it remains true that few, if any, contemporary families can provide the equipment and specialised knowledge required for a modern education, it is plain that the family still performs a fundamental if changed educational role. Although earlier family experiences may be modified or reinforced during the process of formal education, the family nevertheless continues to exert an influence, directly and indirectly, on the development of intelligence, creativity and the motivation to achieve, all of which are fundamental to the effectiveness of the educational process. At a time when evidence of satisfactory performance at school is a principal determinant of occupation and hence also to a large extent of the future pattern of adult life, an understanding of the interaction between the family and the educational system is currently of considerable significance.

Of the conditions conducive to educational attainment, family values, which are reflected in family attitudes to education, have great importance, possibly an overriding importance. Expectations of achievement are different in different social strata. When the goals which can be set realistically differ, so do attitudes to education, which play a part in motivating the child towards the attainment of those goals. In general the higher the family's position in the social hierarchy the more value it accords to education, although there are interesting variations and differing motivations for the respect it enjoys in many strata.

At some levels of the working class a hostile attitude towards education prevails. The middle-class values which permeate the schools, staffed as they are largely by middle-class teachers, are alien values, either not understood, or despised, or unrealistic for a harsher way of life. Education imposes restraints whereas the ethos of lower working-class culture demands immediate satisfactions as manifested by the immediate settlement of disagreements in an aggressive or even violent way, or the immediate purchase of food, drink, or pleasure on the receipt of money. Education, of which little is needed in the types of jobs anticipated, also appears as an incarnation of authority, of 'them', as a virtual extension of the law, or even as a demand which it is smart to evade. Thus irregular attendance is an additional handicap for some whose parents may be too indifferent to rise in time, or whose parents' hostility to authority leads to the magnification of trivial indispositions as excuses for absence. An early, irregular pattern of attendance easily establishes itself as regular truancy when the child is older, by which time he has fallen almost irretrievably behind in his school work.

At many working-class levels a job is for subsistence, to provide for day-to-day necessities, and there is rarely a surplus from which substantial savings could be made. Without assets except the capacity to work, solidarity is a principal value as it is the most effective way of investing a perishable asset profitably. Aspirations tend to be in the direction of security and respectability, except among the most socially depressed or criminal elements. Many jobs do not demand a high degree of literacy, nor the small change of abstractions which are part of the currency of an extended education, and brain work is not regarded as 'real' work but as a soft option. But the upper levels of the working class are now modifying their attitudes. With the superior intelligence and discipline required in their own skilled jobs, enjoying conditions of security and affluence compared with those of the past, and having themselves reaped the benefits of some education, today's parents are aware that selection for the grammar-school type of secondary education is a key to hitherto undreamed-of opportunities for rising in the social hierarchy in a technological age which offers those with some qualifications a good standard of living and a respected place in society. Their attitudes to education now resemble closely and are often indistinguishable from those of the lower middle class, except that the pressure to achieve put upon their children by the latter derives much oftener from a sense of grievance or of disappointment with their own status. Aspiring to the material way of life of the middle class, the upper working-class strata are now beginning to see solidarity with the traditional working class as a threat to their own newer standards, and they no longer share fully its ethos and aspirations.

The striving for upward social mobility is an even more pervasive characteristic underlying middle-class attitudes to education. Although many middle-class families also depend on the product of their labour for their daily bread, needs such as food or clothing are often less immediately urgent, so that more than money alone may be demanded of a job, intrinsic interest and personal satisfaction, for example; and education is valued as an avenue to jobs which can yield these gratifications. This is not to suggest that monetary rewards are despised, which is far from being so. They carry prestige for many reasons. Higher incomes leave a surplus for saving, and the accumulation and expansion of property is a favourite as well as a practicable middle-class pastime, and one which feeds its own appetite for more. Traditional middle-class attitudes to property are, however, changing and some strata now lay their emphasis on lavish spending in a 'we-might-as-well-enjoy-ourselves-while-we-can' manner. But in either circumstance a high income is valued in the middle class and is thus an ambition which colours attitudes to education as a means of attaining it, or of enabling children to remain within the same high income group as their family of origin. For such reasons middle-class demands for educational achievement by the children tend to be more intense than they are in the working class, even when factors such as possible differences in intelligence have been allowed for. Parental aspirations are internalised by the child and may become manifest as competitive, striving and anxious behaviour in relation to school work. Indeed the anxiety about achievement may develop at quite an early age in middle-class children. One six-year-old girl is on record as asking, 'Do you have to take an examination to be a mother?' Such attitudes, it is thought, may well be profitably carried over into the adult world; for the competitiveness, albeit decently concealed, reflects accurately the adult pattern of competition for and in the best possible job, and also the striving for improved social status which is implicit in much middle-class work-activity.[5]

Personal achievement which tends to be seen in terms of upward social mobility can thus be said to be an important societal value in so far as it has relevance for many strata within the middle and working classes. Educational success has become the passport to social mobility, and hence education has become an important value *per se*, although many people make respectable their regard for education by rationalising it as an end in itself 'in its own right'.

The prognosis of achievement

There are many ways in which the family influences performance at school. Each child has an intellectual potential, inherited through the family. But we now know that there is a social component in intelligence, or rather, in the performance by which it is measured, and so heredity does no more than fix certain limits within which social influences may operate. Some of the elements in a child's social environment which affect his performance at school have been isolated and their significance assessed.

It has been shown that material environmental factors affect I.Q. test scores and that the greatest disadvantages in this respect are suffered at the lowest social levels. It might have been expected that a high level of employment together with state social security provision would have ironed out the inequalities which attach to poverty in the race for selective places, but they are still sufficiently evident to be measurable. In the working class generally, the level of housing and other material conditions correlate significantly with the level of test performance at school. As social level rises, material conditions cease to have much effect on performance. So long as the house is warm in winter, comfortably furnished, and not overcrowded, clothing neat, clean and suited to the season, and the diet nutritionally adequate, the child from the detached house, clothed by the top shops, and with a liking for smoked salmon, has as a consequence of his material superiority no advantage in the educational stakes over the child from a semi-detached, dressed with economy, whose most sophisticated taste is for kippers.

In every social class, birth position appears to matter. Only children often do well at school and later in life. Eldest children often do well compared with those born into the same family later, and also better than only children, perhaps because they have the stimulus of competition at home which translates into similarly competitive behaviour at school and work. Youngest children may also become individualists, but they are more likely to suffer from over-protection and they show more symptoms of emotional instability such as nail-biting or unaccountable pains than do their siblings, and these are associated with impaired school performance. No evidence has so far been found to support the hypothesis that because youngest children have certain advantages because of their position in the family they are more likely to attain grammar-school places.[6]

Children from small families have advantages at every social level. The small family environment appears to help children to develop their intelligence and use it optimally. There is more space and more income per head. Parents are able to give them more attention, to talk to them more, so enlarging their vocabularies and giving them an advantage in tests requiring the use of words. In large families the finances and the stamina of the parents are strained, and they tend to be too hard pressed to give each child the support it needs. Furthermore, the relatively poor performance of children from larger families is intensified when they are closely spaced.

In schools which stream their pupils the children of large families are found in the lowest streams in significantly high proportions, together with other children who have had deficient maternal care in the pre-school years. They tend to remain in the streams to which they were originally allocated, which all but destroys their chances of grammar-school places, and later they tend to leave school at the earliest possible date. It would seem that early streaming, or as some have put it, segregation, is social as well as intellectual. The child from the good home and the small family is more likely to be highly streamed. If his home is also in a good neighbourhood, he is more likely to have the opportunities of attending one of the primary schools with a high rate of success in the scramble for grammar-school places. Furthermore, even when the children from the large families and inadequate home environments hold their own in the early school years, their performances deteriorate in the years 8–11, at a time when those of children with favourable home backgrounds are improving.

There is statistical evidence that height and weight and intelligence tend to rise or fall together. There have been attempts to explain the lower I.Q.'s of children from large families in terms of their smaller heights and weights at given ages, and of their delayed physical maturity, but there are now reservations in trying to substantiate a connection between size in childhood and intelligence. Size (the product of diet and heredity) may be of marginal significance compared with lack of space for hobbies, or emotional neglect when parents are constantly overworked, or lack of money for stimulating outings or other activities.

Correlations may indicate statistical probabilities, but with so many subtle influences at work they do not enable us to predict for individuals. Neither are the causal links between the variables clearly identified. However, the findings of all the major studies in this field reach a measure of agreement of the overriding importance of parental attitudes for the child's maximum educational attainment. Parents now realise that they have a role to play in promoting upward social mobility, a role not open to them in societies in which status is more rigidly ascribed, and many make great efforts to enlarge the child's horizons by taking him to 'educational' films and plays and to places of interest in the district and by providing 'improving' reading matter and toys which are demanding, toys which make the child *do* something rather than those complete in themselves, as, indeed, Mrs Beeton was recommending to middle-class parents in 1861 when she protested against giving dolls fully dressed, toy horses ready harnessed, dolls' houses completely furnished in every detail. Some of today's parents will even move house to be within range of a 'good' school. Apparently too they enjoy reading about how to perform their parental role more effectively. In even the cheaper women's magazines, generously interspersed with the horoscopes and knitting patterns, are to be found articles on careers and on child-rearing in all its aspects, including advice on how to cope with the physical and emotional disturbances which may arise at school and lead to under-achievement. And if parents cannot push the child up the social ladder, their tireless efforts may at least prevent him from falling off. For as upward social mobility has become a viable goal for some who would previously have been excluded, similarly for others the threat of downward social mobility, through complacency and lack of educational attainment, has become much more of a reality, particularly at the level of the professional middle class.

To have warm loving parents who show their interest and concern is also a factor favourable to the development of emotional stability in the child, and emotional stability is another factor in successful performance at school. Other things being equal, emotionally disturbed children obtain less than their share of grammar-school places. Nevertheless, some degree of anxiety facilitates achievement, and temporary insecurity, such as that induced by a family move to a new district, may not be detrimental. Very frequent moves in the early years in some circumstances correlate with lower test scores, but families on the move have also been shown to have high achieving children. This is particularly so in the middle class when the ethos of the home is one of competitive striving and the children are without the distractions of a district in which their kinship and friendship roots are deep. Indeed, to have parents who are themselves striving for upward social mobility appears to be an important component in achievement. When the mother works outside the home an element of striving is often present in so far as she is making her effort largely to provide extras for the family, and the children of working mothers used to be high achievers; but so many mothers now work that this correlation is less clear-cut. Similarly, mothers who marry down the social scale sometimes have high achieving children related, it is said, to their discontent with their own reduced status which motivates them to strive themselves and to drive their children to achieve.

Parental pressure and encouragement, from whatever motive, can lead a child to increase his effort, and in all social strata it is the children who work hard who do best, and at all levels of ability performance can be improved by hard work. The hardworking child is usually well behaved in school and well adjusted to life generally, and all these interlocking characteristics are correlated with the degree of parental interest in the child's progress at school.[7] Recent research also suggests that older people can be *taught* to achieve,[8] and this may be exactly what some parents and teachers are doing for the children in their care, that is, they succeed in giving the children motivation, as distinct from mere exhortation and the provision of favourable conditions. Middle-class parents, too, demand more than working-class ones, and middle-class children achieve rather more grammar-school places than their measured intelligence would seem to warrant and working-class children fewer. However, the evidence is not entirely consistent and some investigators have found that every boy who could profit from a grammar-school place in fact receives one, in some districts at least,[9] although it must be remembered here that education authorities vary appreciably in the generosity with which they bestow such places. The degree of 'under-representation' particularly of lower strata of the manual working class increases as the level of the educational institution rises and is at its most marked in the universities, which contain a proportion of 'over-achievers' of the middle class, whose environment better nurtures the social component in the ability to achieve, particularly when the home includes a striving parent. However, the 'striving parent' element can be present in any social stratum, and is quite evident at upper working-class levels, which could also be over-represented. On the present criteria the contention that the middle class is over-represented in selective and higher education is not proven without much more careful definition and scrutiny of the concept of 'over-representation'. What the great volume of research on these topics has done is to draw attention to the probability that family background can be the deciding factor in gaining educational opportunities, particularly when ability is on the borderline.[10]

Given a fair degree of material well-being at home and physical and mental health and warm family care, parental attitudes towards education and parental ambitions for their children have been identified as second only to the quality of the teaching in the primary school, which if it is good can offset some home disadvantages. Children at every level of ability whose parents are easy-going or indifferent do themselves less than justice. But although this is true in general, there are many subtle influences at work moulding parental attitudes to education, and some of the more recent studies have been designed to unravel the processes by which these attitudes translate into the educational performance, successful or otherwise, of their children.

It has been found that fathers who are dissatisfied with their own level of achievement tend to view education as a means of escape for their own children from the frustrations they have themselves experienced, and that their children have a higher success rate in the secondary selective examinations than the children of fathers of a more contented disposition, at the same socio-economic level. Considerable pressures, it seems, are put upon the children so that they become strongly motivated to do well at school. It would appear that the children who do worst of all at school (when allowance has been made for all the variables including intelligence) are those whose fathers are apathetic, unambitious and in jobs without prospects. On the other hand, fathers who have been highly successful in jobs which give them personal satisfaction, and who have moved up the social scale appreciably, do not have the most successful children at school, possibly because they have been too preoccupied with realising their own ambitions to give enough attention and encouragement to their children. Life in the home of a successful father who provides well is also likely to be easy-going. The children may tend to put pleasure before work, simply because there is little deprivation or urgency in their way of life. These matters need further investigation. It could be that the planned deprivations of the prosperous middle-class Victorian nursery and schoolroom—early rising, plain food and insistence on industry and thrift—are an embodiment of the frustrations which may well be among the essential ingredients of achievement.

Certainly there is evidence here and in America that those whose childhoods are conspicuously lacking in both social and parental pressures tend to be without definite goals and hence without the motivation they provide to achieve. An American study in Minnesota traced the histories of children who had been well known as members of pre-school groups more than twenty years earlier, at a time when it was fashionable to encourage children 'to weigh alternatives and to make their own decisions'. The evidence here suggests that children need clear guide lines in doing so. Interesting examples are quoted, for instance of the father who was a 'respected professional man, with a liberal social outlook and a great fondness for his children, but he never stood for anything'. 'He never pressurized one in any way,' his daughter said. He thought 'everyone had a right to his own opinions, ... never said "I told you so" ... or "this is so" ... but always "Well, in my opinion". Mother was real easy-going.' It was concluded from this sort of evidence that 'a person who had a very easy-going permissive childhood revealed a lack of vocational and personal focus in adult life', and 'that to be brought up in an atmosphere in which there are firm beliefs concerning what is acceptable and what is unacceptable is necessary to the person's later well-organised and effective functioning'. Even rules which are resented to some extent are preferable to a complete permissiveness, which the child has not the experience to handle, it was argued. If parents appear indecisive the child tends to become indecisive himself. It is not enough to attempt neutrality; the parent must be committed to a set of personal values if the child is to have clearly defined goals or foci in life. These are necessary in order to promote feelings of personal adequacy. The morality need not be a rigid one, it can develop or be modified, and indeed must do so if it is to remain in touch with the times; but if it is to fulfil its guiding role, it must not shift with every breeze either.[11]

General discipline of a sensible kind contributes towards intellectual achievement, for it inculcates in the child the habit of organising in an orderly way, but *not*, it should be emphasised, an *authoritarian* discipline, which frequently stifles effort and initiative. It is the family with a democratic ethos, enabling children to participate in decision-making guided and encouraged but not bulldozed by sensible, firm, friendly parents, which appears, so far as the evidence goes, to foster achievement motivation.

At present, informed opinion inclines to the view that the conventionally 'happy' home supplies a poor spur to effort, that it is not enough for the parent to provide emotional warmth, a sheltered environment free from material anxieties, with books and toys readily available for the child to select an appropriate activity at his own pace. His own pace tends to be slower, and sometimes appreciably slower, than the pace he could achieve in a more stimulating family milieu. However, studies of the influence of parental attitudes and other home circumstances favourable to the educational achievement of children are still far from sophisticated, so that inferences drawn from these generalisations must be treated with caution as they may well be modified in the light of further research. The one inescapable general conclusion is that when ability is borderline, family background can tip the scales for or against gaining access to the educational opportunities that are increasingly essential for job-success in later life.

Part III

The family life developmental cycle

The family life developmental cycle

Credit for identifying and conceptualising the family life cycle must go to Charles Booth and Seebohm Rowntree who in their late nineteenth-century studies of poverty in London and York were able to show that life experience and expectation vary in accordance with clearly defined stages in the life cycle. The family life cycle has now become one of the accepted conceptual frameworks[1] in use among family sociologists to facilitate their attempts to identify and explain the social influences on family behaviour. From this perspective the examination of the nuclear family as a small social group becomes more dynamic, changing relationships within the family being viewed as a series of role changes which are related to the developmental tasks appropriate to each stage in the family life cycle. Throughout the cycle there is a gradual and continuous change of roles and hence of statuses also, and each succeeding role-status change demands a series of adjustments from members of the group. By reorganising our thinking to incorporate insights from the life cycle theory, we add a new dimension to our understanding of the family.

A new family is founded when a couple sign the marriage register and that family completes its cycle when both are dead. The time which elapses between the wedding bells and the funeral rites clearly varies for individual couples, but a young couple usually expects to pass through a 'normal' developmental cycle. This means that there will be an initial period without children; a period in which life is intensively child–centred and which lasts until the youngest child goes to school; a period when adolescents are being launched into the world, becoming established in their careers and ultimately founding their own families; a period in middle life when the original couple are again on their own, and which is often a period of relative prosperity; a period of retirement, old age, widowhood and at last the death of the survivor. Although they may fuse imperceptibly into one another, each of these stages has clearly defined characteristics, each requires the performance of certain *developmental tasks* as they have been called (some of which have been discussed in Part II) and each successive stage demands appropriate adjustments from members of the group. The whole cycle is characterised by gradual expansion, followed by gradual contraction. Within the general outline of growth and shrinkage are innumerable intermediary patterns with identifiable characteristics, such as families with several wage earners, families without a breadwinner, childless couples and so on, all of which differing situations affect the texture of family life. So role changes also involve adjustments to a sequence which may not follow the expected 'normal' pattern.

The family life cycle concept embraces the idea that not only is the family a small group of interacting personalities but also that this small group interacts with an institutional structure. By facilitating the analysis of changes in roles to meet differing needs, tasks and responsibilities at each stage of family development, which are numerous and continual in a family of any size, it can help to clarify and explain both the intra- and extra-familial conditions in which the changes take place. Role changes frequently bring tensions which can precipitate family disorganisation of varying degrees of intensity as, for example, when the onset of adolescence is accompanied by generation conflict, and some crises may be so severe that they lead to total disruption in the form of divorce or death. Adjustments are always required to stress, conflict and crisis situations both within the family group and between the family and the external social structure. Thus the family cycle concept has great significance in the study of family welfare and hence for social policy-making also.

The sections which follow will examine selected aspects of the life cycle as family change in process. In them we shall look more closely at some of the specific family situations which in our society give rise to anxiety and potentially to crisis, and relate them to sociological knowledge about the family. Some of these situations, for example courtship, marriage, birth, retirement, death and widowhood, fall to the lot of a high proportion of family members, and in this sense most of these can be regarded as normal, and some of them as almost unavoidable experiences. Other situations such as divorce, violent generation conflict or extreme poverty, are disruptive and in some cases preventable, and they do not form part of newly-weds' hopes or expectations, so we shall try later to discover why some families fail to cope with the tensions which arise either as a result of role changing, or which are a consequence of situations and events in the larger society, or which may be a function of the interaction of the two.

Adolescent stresses and conflicts

The presence of adolescents or young adults under the parental roof has a recurring association with family stress, so much so that some authorities regard it as 'normal' in our culture. The erstwhile children are being established in the world and preparing to take on adult roles; the ageing parents are being gradually superannuated from the more strenuous family roles. The conflicts which arise in the continuum from total dependence to total independence are accentuated and may enter an acute phase when the young people covet the privileges of adulthood without the assumption of its responsibilities and self-discipline; their parents, on the other hand, must solve the problems which arise in acquiescing to a different set of values and of 'letting go' while at the same time protecting their fledglings from the consequences of their inexperience. This situation is pregnant with possibilities of strife, concealed or overt, and is in some degree potentially disruptive.

The assumption of adult roles brings concomitant changes in status which are sometimes clearly heralded by some signal such as the début of an upper-class girl into 'society'. But for most there is no one event which marks the emergence from childhood to adulthood, no prescribed rituals such as take place at puberty in many simpler societies. Although the change in status is usually gradual and without a set pattern it links most closely but not exclusively with economic independence. A combination of physical, intellectual and emotional maturity is also ideally prescribed in our society. Physical maturity is relatively easily observed and seemingly takes place at ever earlier ages.[2] But intellectual maturity, if this means the full development of an individual's potential, is circumscribed or denied to many by lack of opportunity, while for others it may require long years of effort and an artificially prolonged dependence. Emotional maturity is a very complex concept difficult though not impossible to measure, but there can be little doubt from the incidence of neurotic illness alone that it is not easy of achievement. All in all, the attainment of adult status is easiest to recognise if it is looked at solely from the point of view of the functioning and maintenance of society. Societal continuity requires, principally, economic effort and the replacement of its members, and from this viewpoint, an adult is one who contributes fully to economic activity and who has also founded a family which will provide replacements in the next generation.[3]

At adolescence masculine and feminine roles have to be internalised and the proper behaviour assumed before adult status is fully accorded, and those who deviate from the expected adult pattern are ostracised or punished in other ways. In contemporary society the achievement of appropriate sex identification arouses more conflict than in the past when roles were less fluid. American evidence suggests that highly educated girls who know themselves to be the intellectual equals or superiors of certain men nevertheless still feel obliged to adopt attitudes of deference towards those men. The belief that a girl is well advised to hide her cleverness, that a man will not marry a blue-stocking, dies hard. It would seem, too, that women are more often dissatisfied with feminine roles than are men with masculine roles, so it may be that an adolescent girl has greater adjustments to make than has a boy. Possibly sex identification is made no easier for her by the fact that it is more socially acceptable for a girl to mimic the appearance and behaviour of men than the reverse. The young men currently flaunting colourful frilly blouses, scent, ear-rings and a profusion of jangling necklaces would probably, even now, be arrested if they added skirts also. Girls, on the other hand, can with impunity usurp most of the visible symbols of manhood—trousers, twig-like silhouette, smoking, the list is long—with the exception of the beard; few achieve even a moustache, and that rather late in life. The convention that the male plays an active part and the female a passive part in mate selection is a further source of anxiety to some adolescent girls in a society which increasingly pays lip service to the idea of sexual equality.

There are always personality adjustments to be made at adolescence, and the cultural and other stresses which frequently cause difficulty have a wide distribution over time, space and socio-economic developmental level. The adolescent must come to terms with the discontinuities of cultural expectations, identified by Ruth Benedict in 1938. The son eventually becomes the father, and in our society this means that one who has been expected to be pliant, to accept parental authority, to acquiesce in major decisions made on his behalf, must reverse his attitudes and assume the dominant role when he founds his own family. From being excluded by law from any but the most marginal economic activity in childhood, he must become chief provider. A carefree childhood is followed by a whole spectrum of responsibilities. The extent of cultural discontinuities found varies. Less drastic personal adjustments are demanded in societies in which, for example, the roles of father and son are less differentiated and the father has a companionable relationship with the son and encourages in him the development of the qualities needed in the father-provider role, such as reasonable aggression; or in societies in which children from the time they can walk are given tasks which have genuine economic usefulness for the group and are suited to their capacities at each stage of development. In a highly technological culture such as our own it is not easy to arrange that children should be continually and responsibly participant, and it has been suggested that we provide inadequate socialisation compared with some primitive communities, that we do less through our institutional arrangements to mitigate the strains involved in moving from role to role, and that failure in this respect exacerbates the tensions which are evident at this time.

In societies whose culture permits the assumption of adult roles early, the transition from child to adult is usually smooth. In our own society, adult status is accorded early in the lower socio-economic strata, and appears to be a less traumatic experience, on the whole, than in middle-class strata. Formal education often ends as soon as the legal minimum age for leaving school is reached, and earnings soon approach those of the unskilled adult worker, so that the working-class adolescent more frequently achieves an early economic independence. He (and she) also tends to be more sexually experienced [4] and early marriage more frequently follows than in the middle class, so the working-class child more often soon achieves two important determinants of adult status, full economic independence and independent family life.

In our society the adolescent has a cultural need to identify with his peer group. The gap between generations now seems at its widest, parental standards being rejected to a greater or lesser degree. Appearances are indicative of the depth of the chasm; the 'short back and sides' of the father contrast oddly with the long silken tresses of his son, and the flower-hatted pearl-bedecked mother with the compelling, casual anti-grooming of her daughter. Attitudes tend to be similarly polarised. Children may see parents as conservative, cautious and repressive; to parents children may appear unresponsive and rebellious. Children wish to assert their independence, parents to cushion them from the hazards of launching when choices are made of careers, friends and leisure pursuits which will affect their whole lives. They want their children to be accepted by the wider society (unless they themselves are members of a deviant sub-culture) and acceptance requires submission to societal norms, which are not always those of the peer group, which may, for a time, be anti-societal in its normative behaviour; and to the adolescent the approval of his contemporaries may seem more important than that of his parents and of society, which is symbolised by parental authority.

In an era when standards of behaviour at all ages and at all social levels are in a state of flux, the moral dilemma of adolescents, in the absence of fixed codes, is greater than for past generations when most were well aware of what was expected and conformed outwardly at least to conventional expectations. Adults, and parents in particular, are frequently sources of frustration. The adolescent is ready for sexual experience and possibly for marriage, but the social norms are still on the whole hostile to both, particularly in the social strata which put a high value on education. So he must first be trained to make his way in the world and it falls to parents to persuade him that adolescence in our society is a preparation for life. The teenage culture, from which parents are excluded, is in part a response to these conflicts and frustrations, to the denial by society of gratifications now within reach. With its adolescent norms and status hierarchy—the pop idols, the coffee bars, the 'fancy-dress' clothes—it is said to represent an institutionalised protest against the restraints of authority. Its most favourable incubation medium is where family ties are loose and discipline slack. There is no place for a 'youth cult' in a peasant society, where the family is not only the principal occupational outlet, which as we have seen demands a hierarchical structure of authority, but is necessarily the main focus of social life also.

The parents' dilemma in contemporary society is seemingly insoluble. Those who attempt to 'stay young' and adopt the styles, speech and interests of a younger generation are an embarrassment to their children. If they are wholly pliable, their children have nothing to rebel against, which some psychologists regard as a need at adolescence, and their permissiveness may be regarded as disinterestedness and encourage the very behaviour they deprecate. Over-solicitousness in parents, on the other hand, may stifle the urge to independence, which is to do their children a disservice. But in spite of the difficulties, tolerance frequently reappears later, and a remarkable number of families seem to emerge unscathed if we can judge by the number of young married couples (and not only of the working class, though there is less evidence for other classes) who choose to live near the parental home, or who declare they would do so if local authority policy in the allocation of tenancies permitted it. In the Dagenham development, for example, in the years before the war when it was easier to get houses, daughters chose to settle near their mothers and kinship networks emerged not dissimilar to those in a traditional working-class area. And even in situations in which the cultural gap is wide, for example when well-educated achievers outstrip their under-educated parents, empirical surveys both here and in America show that later there is frequently a warm relationship between the generations (see Ch. 3).

It seems that generation conflict is less likely at adolescence in homogeneous sub-cultures than it is when the young rub shoulders with all sorts as in a comprehensive school or a university, where parental standards have to stand more comparisons and are more likely to be challenged. In such circumstances peer approval often demands some modification of hitherto unquestioned ways of behaving as when, for example, middle-class adolescents adopt pseudo-backstreet voices in a bid for more general peer acceptance. Thus it would appear that the greatest degree of parental–adolescent harmony is likely to be found among close-knit ethnic or religious groups, and in suburbs where families are of roughly the same socio-economic and educational background. Family life in such circumstances is in some measure insulated from alien influences. When certain aspects of the general teenage culture permeate such groups, for example, parties after parties or uninvited guests, it is among adolescents whose parents 'speak the same language' and who therefore have been exposed to conditioning influences which are not widely different; a situation wholly dissimilar from that in the 'melting pot' of the megalopolis.

A smooth transition to adult roles is likely to be easiest when childhood and adult roles are not too different and when ultimate goals are seen in the same terms by the generations. It is also probable when there is some external societal pressure to keep the young to heel such as depression, unemployment, expectation of inheritance, deep religious beliefs which emphasise duty to parents or ancestors, or when there is a strong societal expectation that a child will follow in the parental footsteps. These are for the most part characteristics of a stabler, more static society than our own. In a dynamic society, the aspirations of child and parent tend to become out of alignment. Attractive alternatives become available, distaste for the values and occupation of the previous generation becomes exaggerated. There are also alternative founts of wisdom in a complex society where parental experience and knowledge of opportunities is circumscribed; the teacher, for example, may stand *in loco parentis* in some respects.

Although there are many visible and measurable manifestations of the challenge to the older generation in our society, the conclusion reached from the evidence of a survey of 250 15–18-year-old young workers of both sexes in London (the sort of group in which peer-influence tends to be maximised) is of interest.

Throughout this research it is clear that an overwhelming majority of these young people have a high valuation of marriage and family life. Many pay spontaneous tributes to what their families have been able to give them, and show an appreciation of the difficulties their parents often had to contend with. They envisage their own future in terms of a happy marriage and a family.[5]

It seems, then, that feelings of solidarity are not inconsistent with the partial rejection of the parental family as a normative reference.[6] There are some who maintain that we labour the difficulties encountered at adolescence too much, and that the attitude of the middle-class Victorians, who regarded it as something to be got through without fuss, had much to commend it. Perhaps it was easier for them in an era, solid and self-confident, when goals were clear-cut, progress seemingly assured and with time available to admire their own backbones, on which, as they firmly believed, the structure of national prosperity was so steadfastly supported. Many of the stresses of adolescence about which we hear so much are not only cultural and psychological in origin, but are the product of changed economic conditions.

Courtship

Courtship is a dominant interest of young people of both sexes. Sometimes the intention is to engage in only transitory relationships, but for the majority courtship ultimately finds its fruition in marriage. The norms of courtship reflect those of marriage in a society or stratum of a society. In general the selection of a marriage partner is today more a matter of personal preference than it has been in most other epochs of human history; and perhaps the greater freedom of choice has brought in its train more tensions than might have been encountered when courtship was regulated in accordance with explicit and accepted criteria. In Britain only incestuous marriages are banned. There is indeed an almost universal taboo on incest, and where it has been institutionalised, as for example in the royal house of ancient Egypt, the limits have been carefully defined. In some societies rules are precise and strict, particularly in those which are rigidly hierarchical and have highly functional families. The most frequently imposed rules are those which prescribe either *exogamy*, i.e. marriage outside a particular social group, or *endogamy*, i.e. marriage within a particular social group. It is the more open societies, in which the family is relatively functionless, which tend to leave the choice of mate to the couple concerned, and the basis is often one of mutual attraction alone in a society such as our own with personal happiness as the principal goal in marriage. The more highly functional the family is within a social structure the more likely it is also that marriages will be arranged or that parents will have a substantial say. In a peasant economy, for example, a bride with a suitable dowry may be sought to add to the family resources; or a bride who is strong and healthy, who can help with farm work and bear numerous children and so ensure continuity in the next generation, or who is domesticated enough to feed and look after the men who do the heavy work on the farm. Or marriage may be dynastic, that is, it is intended to merge opposing interests or to consolidate property, and marriages of this kind are common in highly stratified societies. In all such cases individual preference assumes less importance than the welfare of the group. The arranged marriage is now rare, although some settlements and trust funds have similarities to dowries, bride prices and the like.

Nevertheless, even when romantic love is the socially approved detonator to the decision to marry, the family position in society effectively circumscribes the field of choice. In a modern society, such as Britain, there is a 'field of eligibles', and although the rules of courtship are flexible, the mores nevertheless inhibit marriages which cross barriers of age, race, religion, class or education. There is pressure towards endogamous marriage.

Marriage is regarded by some as a vehicle of social mobility, but the amount of mobility which actually takes place by this means is limited, regardless of sex, because of the difficulties of exploring the territory outside the usual 'field of eligibles'. But there are more opportunities for doing so than in the past. The old way of maintaining status in the upper class or of improving status in the middle class by way of an advantageous marriage is no longer wholly viable. Arranging social occasions to provide opportunities for 'suitable' young people to meet is still a principal activity of the upper- and middle-class matron, but the mother's function, and hence her influence, in finding marriage partners for her children is much reduced in these strata, and as a consequence the matron has become a less powerful figure within the family group, unless some of her other activities are such as will add to her authority. The situation is intensified for the career-centred middle class by the dispersal of the kingroup, that ready-made source of social invitations, which is still effectively used by the upper class in the mating game. In the working-class complex kinship networks still survive within the same town or district, and for its geographically less mobile young people, 'the girl next door' remains a popular choice which in its turn serves to perpetuate these local kingroups. Accordingly, it can be seen that young people in different social strata are 'exposed', as the Americans put it, to different opportunities for mate selection in respect of class mores, the degree of kinship interaction and of physical mobility. The advent of selective education on the basis of performance has enabled some to disregard the old barriers, and two world wars have also eased social mixing.

When social movement takes place as a result of marriage, men are more likely than women to marry 'down'. Because a woman takes her husband's status he 'raises' her, as when the surgeon marries the nurse of possibly lower social origin, or the business executive his secretary. She is acceptable to his friends because she is his wife. A man can raise his status by his own efforts to take his wife with him. On the other hand, the woman who marries 'down' does not raise her husband to her level, she descends herself, for he is less likely to be acceptable to her former friends and acquaintances. It is much rarer for a man to succeed in climbing socially by means of his higher-status wife; marriage to the boss's daughter, never common, is still, as it probably has been always, mainly in the realms of fiction. A girl with money and position is no doubt sought after, again as she always has been, but there is no reason to believe that she, and her parents, are less averse than in the past to attempting to use position to augment her fortune and ensure her comfort. Parents are unlikely to encourage her to lavish *their* often hard-won assets on someone who cannot hope to keep her in the same style. Conversely, looks and a few social graces, although they help, other things being equal, are not now necessarily enough to attract the clever young man. Today he is likely to expect more of a prospective wife, such as expert knowledge in some field. Perhaps her potential earning power may influence him in an age when it is becoming the norm for married women to work outside the home. He cannot be unaware of the fact that he can in effect double his income the moment he signs the marriage register if his bride has a similar qualification to his own, whereas his colleague who marries 'down' virtually halves his; for if this bride continues her lower status and possibly ill-paid occupation, she detracts from her husband's status and prospects also. It would appear that the girl who merely aspires to fill in a few years at some genteel job before marriage is now at a disadvantage compared with the past, unless she has a personal fortune behind her. And at a time when more girls are being educated beyond the minimum school leaving age, it follows that there are more young women with qualifications of one kind or another around than ever before, so that marriage to such a girl is now a possible and even prudent proposition.

Although in an open society inter-stratum marriage is easier, the majority still marry into the same or an adjacent class to a significantly greater extent than would occur by chance, and an examination of marriage cohorts since the turn of the century has shown only a slight decline in the degree of class endogamy.[7] The stratum most likely to make unexpected marriages is that of the skilled manual worker; they are least likely at the professional and managerial level. Those with a university or higher education also show a high degree of assortive mating, although the social origins of the couples may be diverse. It is rare for marriage partners to be of both different educational background and different social origin. It would thus appear from the statistical evidence that original ascribed family status, modified by later educational experience, plays a major part in determining subsequent selection of a mate.

Courtship behaviour varies widely. In Britain promiscuity is frowned on, as it is in most known societies, but courtship practices differ and may include some sexual experiment. Many studies show that there is a wide range in the degree to which individuals are sexually involved outside marriage, both before and after, and that social class is a significant variable, so much so that extra-marital sexual involvement is one of the secondary indicators of class-status position. In general, working-class boys and girls, who often live in cramped conditions and have sexual knowledge at an early age as a result, are more likely to have total sex experience than their middle-class counterparts, who although they may experiment in a greater variety of ways, more often stop short of totality. There are sex differences in attitudes to premarital sexual activity, too. Men of all classes treat sexual experience comparatively lightly, as an end in itself, a seal on their 'manhood', as a means of personal fulfilment, and they use the 'right' to 'freedom' for 'fulfilment' as a perennial argument in persuading girls to co-operate. Women have been shown to be less casual in their attitudes, much more emotionally involved in the experience, and they usually sincerely believe themselves to be 'in love'. By contrast the male protestations of 'love' are plausible, but not infrequently prove transient. Women sense this and survey material in both England and America suggests that few genuinely want the sexual freedom demanded by some feminists, 'sexual equality with men' as it has been put.

It should perhaps be remarked in passing that many of the early feminists in demanding sexual equality aimed to raise male standards of fidelity not to depress female ones. Currently, although sexual morals vary greatly by social stratum, some of the most vociferous champions of 'female sexual equality' are men, for whom fornication and adultery became pleasanter when there is an 'emancipated' supply of amateurs, cheaper than maintaining a 'love nest', and less risky than consorting with prostitutes.

There are indeed no socially acceptable ways of satisfying the urgent sexual drives of late adolescence. The 'trial' or 'companionate' marriage, advocated by Havelock Ellis more than thirty years ago, has never received societal sanction, so experiment takes place clandestinely with varying degrees of completeness. Most women seem to seek a recognised and preferably continuing relationship with one man, but societal arrangements are such that men may continue to shop around where opportunity beckons. As some American writers have put it, women are 'person-centred' while men tend to be 'body-centred' except in regard to their own groups of eligible marriage partners. Societal mores do not facilitate the feminine preference; new social habits make it more difficult than before for a girl to see and pursue her own interests.

The most exhaustive studies there are of premarital sexual behaviour are American, and U.S. college students' sexual lives and attitudes have been examined in great detail. In this setting it has been shown that class barriers are rarely crossed even in extra-marital sexual activity, and that among the minority who have sexual experience outside their own class, men cross class barriers downwards, women upwards. The women are often hoping for marriage as the ultimate outcome, but as marriage tends to be endogamous, their hopes are rarely justified. Men, and particularly those of the middle class it appears from this evidence, still tend to 'respect' women they regard as suitable marriage partners, and do not engage in total sex relationships with them. They also 'respect' those whom they genuinely love, of whatever class. They may attempt to involve girls of a higher stratum but not usually with much success, although sometimes they do 'trap' them into marriage. Indeed, the ever-present possibility of an unwanted extra-marital pregnancy followed by a disadvantageous marriage is one of the reasons why parents of substance like to see their daughters 'suitably' married at an early age.

Gorer found that with the exception of the lower working class the majority of English people favoured the strictest standards of chastity outside marriage, that a great many of them lived up to their ideals and that the young were particularly rigid in these attitudes.[8] There is a general belief that extra-marital sexual involvement has been increasing in recent years. Although precise information is available for limited groups only, such a belief is given substance by a marked increase in illegitimate births in the sixties.[9] The amount of venereal disease, which is significantly correlated with irregular sexual relationships, has, according to official sources,[10] also increased alarmingly, indeed to 'epidemic' proportions.

Marriage itself is traditionally regarded as one of life's turning points, and its solemnity is marked in most communities by ritual with its own symbolism such as the bride dressed in white to denote purity, and the unbroken circle of the wedding ring underlining the eternal or permanent nature of the vows taken. The role changes are greater in some societies than in others. On the whole the greater the change the more elaborate and prolonged the ceremony and honeymoon, thus emphasising the change and giving both the couple and their families an interval in which to adjust to a new situation with new roles. Today marriage for a girl may mean not so much the assumption of new roles as simply the addition of another dimension to a set of roles that already exists and which she will continue to perform. She may already have been living independently of her family of origin, she may have experienced a degree of sexual involvement, she may be returning to the office on Monday, she may mean to continue to enjoy financial independence. If girls with this outlook increase in number ceremonial is likely to simplify still further, which (in addition to the increase of secular attitudes in society) accounts in part for the growth of registry office ceremonies. Today's new marriage partners initially perform what are as much simply masculine and feminine roles as marriage roles.

For most women today it is motherhood which heralds a sharp break with the past, the role change from working girl to housewife. Most then give up work for a time unless there is real financial hardship or exceptional career-dedication. It is now that the flat is exchanged for the house; that leisure-time activities become home-centred. A dog follows the baby and in due course guinea-pigs, rabbits, goldfish. Money becomes tighter with mortgage or other payments to be met out of an income depleted by the loss of the girl's earnings. Do-it-yourself, born of necessity, is elevated to a hobby. Additions are made to the demesne, sheds, cupboards, rabbit hutches and dolls houses, for it is likely that the husband, too, will participate actively in the home-making activities. If more babies follow, the domestic role for the wife will consist of baby care, shopping, cooking, housework, accompanying children to and from school, budgeting, and preventing the domestic animals from actually dying of starvation when their youthful owners are forgetful. Her diversions will be talking to other mothers at the school gate or at tea parties, and perhaps a hobby other than sewing and dressmaking if she is strong minded. If she resists or rebels against this expected pattern, role strain or even role conflict will arise, as they do with the working wife discussed earlier, and as they will also if she does not observe the expected norms of child-rearing for her class or neighbourhood.

As we have seen in Ch. 2, compared with those of more tightly structured societies, contemporary marriage goals are indefinite. Expectations, too, are often unrealistically romantic compared with the reality described above and they are also highly individual, for there is often no clear perception of what is involved. The meaning of 'love' is ambiguous in the minds of many of those about to marry, and some analyses have shown that couples who think they have found 'love' actually mean they feel secure. Attitudes to 'sex' are muddled, and although outside marriage it is widely disapproved, with egocentric values prominent, practice is not altogether in accord with precept in complex societies, as Kinsey and others have shown. Thus personal happiness as a principal goal tends to be vague and insubstantial and to demand the reconciliation of possibly irreconcilable ideals.

The American sociologist, Kingsley Davis, takes a gloomy view of modern marriage. Modern marriage, he says, is mainly a 'vehicle for sexual gratification and companionship. Outside this sphere, it has no significance that would give it stability.' 'If,' he continues, 'marriage does not somehow involve the partners in common activities . . . apart from sexual intercourse, it cannot hope to produce a satisfactory companionship or attain any stability. . . . The instability of modern marriage clearly shows that it is becoming deficient as a source of emotional security.' [1] Readers will notice in these passages the conviction that modern marriage *is* unstable, but opinions are divided about this. It is undeniable that the institutional functions of the family have declined in importance (see Ch. 2) except for the reproductive and socialising ones, which have always been and still are central, and that affection and companionship have emerged as of great importance to the new concept of marriage. But some writers see this as a strength rather than a weakness, and one of the currently acceptable views in relation to modern Britain has been summed up by Ronald Fletcher, who states that 'the "essential" functions of the family centred upon sexual relationships, parenthood and home-making, are fulfilled far more satisfactorily in the modern family than they were in the family of the distant or the recent past'. Fletcher maintains in his conclusions that his analysis lends support to his thesis that 'the family in contemporary Britain has not declined in nature or importance as a social institution; that its characteristics do not warrant at all the charge of moral decline'.[2] O. R. McGregor, too, argues for reasons indicated later that the increase in divorce rates does not necessarily indicate a decline in the importance of the family nor in its stability.[3]

When asked, most couples categorise themselves as happily married. Many such marriages are happy in the negative sense that overt conflict is kept under control and that there are some common interests such as children or a profession. But a total sharing of all aspects of life in an active rather than a passive relationship is much rarer, so it would seem from American evidence which is more detailed than that available for Britain specifically. The usual marital adjustment measurement scales classify as 'successful' those marriages in which the couple engage in little open conflict, have a fair degree of agreement on major issues, have similar interests, share some of their leisure time, and have an affection for one another. Such marriages may contain little emotional warmth; they may abound with resentments and suppressed conflict, and exist on an accommodation basis rather than an interaction one, on habit rather than enthusiastic cooperation.

Crisis situations in families can take numerous forms, but the most readily perceptible is marriage break-up and its consequences. We must distinguish between marriage breakdown, which is a process, and marriage break-up, between family disorganisation which may be only trivial, a consequence of temporary failure of marital adjustment, and family disintegration. But all these are always regarded seriously for they constitute a threat to the institution of the family and, through the family, to the structure and functioning of society itself, in so far as society is dependent upon the family for the nurture and socialisation of its future members. Thus the conflicts between husband and wife which may be the harbingers of desertion, separation or divorce, are more than the private concerns of two ill-mated individuals.

There are identifiable patterns of family disorganisation which may or may not precede marriage break-up, and influences which make it difficult or impossible for individuals to conform to the norms and rules of the marriage relationship, and which may also be related to more general social changes. Social change has been particularly rapid and radical in the twentieth century. Industrialisation and urbanisation have intensified. In the train of two world wars has come a free and informal relationship between the sexes. The status of women has improved and the new opportunities for work outside the home means that they do not feel irrevocably tied to a dead marriage as their sole means of support. An all-pervasive technology has fathered, for example, central heating and the zip-fastener, which in their turn have made brief, provocative, quickly-divested clothing practicable. Easier transport has facilitated clandestine meetings and undermined the traditional forms of social control. The permutations of these and similar themes are infinite and momentous, and an increasing divorce rate has kept pace showing a consistently upward trend not only in absolute numbers (a misleading measure), but also in proportion to the number of marriages at risk. Its association with the intensification of industrialisation in all its aspects would hardly be in doubt were it not for the fact that a very intensive growth of industrialisation in Japan was accompanied by a *falling* divorce rate, which means that marriage in Japan has become more, not less, stable.[4] Moslem countries, backward in industrialisation, also tend to have high divorce rates.

Considerable weight, therefore, must be given not only to changes in attitudes to the permanence and sanctity of marriage which may be a product of industrialisation, but also to legislative and administrative changes (themselves a reflection of those new attitudes) as among the significant factors which have contributed to the break-up, if not the breakdown, of marriages in Britain. The grounds for divorce in England and Wales have widened, in the first instance by putting women on an equality with men (after 1923 it was no longer necessary for a woman petitioner to prove cruelty as well as adultery) and then in 1937 when grounds other than adultery were introduced and the 'respectable' divorce was possible for the first time. A new Divorce Reform Bill is currently before Parliament, and if it becomes law 'irretrievable breakdown' of a marriage will become the sole ground for divorce. Although this proposal is hedged by many restrictions, the effect would be to increase the availability of divorce to some who were previously excluded. It would, for example, make divorce possible when both spouses are agreeable after two years of waiting, and at the wish of one only after five years. Procedures have also been progressively simplified and cheapened, so bringing the possibility of divorce within the reach of ever wider categories of people. Historically, as each obstacle has been modified, there has typically been an upward swing in the number of petitions presented in the years immediately after the change, followed by a levelling off to a new 'normal' figure somewhat higher than the previous one, a pattern observable since 1857.[5]

Some of the increase can be accounted for by the trend to obtain a divorce rather than a legal separation, the latter formerly being the only way out of an unsatisfactory marriage for the poor. Part, however, can be explained demographically, for the divorce figures to some extent reflect the changing age structure of the population. More than half of all divorces involve marriages of more than ten years standing, 30 per cent involve marriages of more than fifteen years standing, and in the past some of these marriages would have been ended by death before reaching breaking point, so that some contemporary divorces are merely the product of longer life expectancy. The chances of marriage have been increasing too since the Second World War for both sexes and for all ages under 55, so there are also more marriages at risk.[6]

Divorce rates are comparatively high between childless and one-child couples who have been married for some years. Apart from early marriages, these are the marriages most at risk. Approximately one-third of all divorcees are childless,[7] but it cannot be assumed that child-lessness is in itself a precipitating or causative factor. American studies have shown that it is not the fact of having children which makes for success in marriage, but that it *is* important that the couple should genuinely hold the same views about having children. In these circum-stances it appears that childless couples are as well adjusted as the rest, and that the absence of children does not affect the stability of the marriage when there is a wish for children but none are born. It is the desire for children which is correlated with both the stability and the 'success' of the marriage. A finding of this kind provides a step, how-ever small, towards an explanation of the processes at work, and is a good illustration of the superficiality of some of the inferences which are often made from demographic and other statistical data. Clearly childlessness can be a cause of dissension in marriage, but the extent to which this is so and the reasons cannot be inferred from official statistics alone.

Children, wanted or unwanted, may in some cases also be sources of conflict, but so far as the evidence goes, the natural bonds between parent and child appear to provide an area of mutual involvement for the parents in which they can lay aside their own disagreements in constructive, mutual concern for the welfare of the children. Certainly the presence of children has been shown to inhibit the initiation of divorce proceedings, and some marriages then continue to survive beyond the point when the immediate needs of the children are rele-vant. There is, however, an increasing tendency for couples with chil-dren to resort to divorce. More than the *desired* number appear to cause discord.[8] The most that can be said perhaps on the relationships between children and the success of marriage is that the evidence is contradictory. American studies tend to show that childless marriages are happy in the early years, but that after five or more years those with one or more children score better on the 'marriage success' scales.

133

Also significant when considering the most recent upward movement is the habit of marrying at younger ages which has been evident during and since the war.[9] Most divorces take place between the ages of 25 and 35 (regardless of sex), and when the whole range is taken into account, the marriages most at risk are those of 4–9 years duration, inclusive. The risk to these marriages is intensified if the bride was under 20 at the time of the marriage. When the figures are analysed on the basis of the age of the bride and the duration of the marriage, the most divorce-prone women are seen to be those who married under 20 and have experienced 4–6 years of married life; and the incidence of divorce in these groups is even higher than the large figures suggest because the peak years for marriage are somewhat later. For brides who married under 20 the divorce rates remain high; whatever the length of the marriage they remain consistently more than double the rates for women who married in the age range 20–24, firm evidence it would seem of the instability of youthful marriages. They have also potentially longer to run which in itself increases the probability that they will reach the divorce courts.

It should be remembered that age at marriage varies by social class. Early marriage is practicable when maximum earnings are reached early, as they are among unskilled workers, or where, as in the upper class, income is unearned or when the family of origin supports the young couple. Traditionally the middle class and those with middle-class aspirations delayed marriage until some qualifications had been acquired which would enable the maintenance of a middle-class style of life. The present middle-class preference to marry between 22 and 24 is younger than was the practice a generation ago, and this change is related to the easier financial circumstances as a consequence of grants for higher education, more certainty of finding employment after the completion of education and the more ready social acceptance of the wife working for a period after marriage. All this contrasts with the position before the war when professional men, particularly those aspiring to the upper reaches of the law or medicine, for example, were dependent on their own or their parents' resources until their late twenties, and when the purchase of an appropriate house and its contents seemed a necessary preliminary to marriage. Sometimes, too, there were frustrating prohibitions on marriage, as in the case of those bank clerks who were expected to remain unwed until the age of 28.

In any class early marriage can still give rise to later frustrations. It can be a barrier to progress in education or occupation, dissipating energy which could otherwise be concentrated on the job in hand. Low income is a hindrance to marital adjustment and this is often an accompaniment of youthful marriage. Premarital pregnancy is also a contraindication, and is again associated with youth. Nearly one-third of all brides are pregnant on their wedding day and the highest rates of pregnancy before marriage are among the youngest brides.[10] Some of these marriages are no doubt of the 'shot-gun' variety consequent upon parental and other social pressures, which means that they are the result of chance rather than of choice, although pregnant brides frequently maintain that the only effect of the pregnancy is to bring into being earlier an intended marriage. Nevertheless, 'shot-gun' marriages produce a higher than average proportion of ill-assorted couples. Furthermore, premarital sexual involvement even without pregnancy following, and bearing in mind that there are wide differences in the motivations for and the circumstances of sexual involvement before marriage, is a negative predictor of future harmony. It has been shown that those who have had lax sexual standards before marriage even with a fiancé(e) are more likely to be unfaithful after, and adultery is another variable known to put a severe strain on most marriages in which it occurs, with few exceptions.

Position in the family may be important. Marriage between two only children does not always turn out well. The only child has more than the usual number of adjustments to make on marriage, having had the totality of parental attention and less opportunity for sharing. In terms of statistical probability it appears that the outlook for a stable, happy marriage is better when neither, or only one, partner is an only child. This of course is merely one of the ways in which the experiences of early life affect patterns of behaviour in later life; and not necessarily only for one generation for experience is passed on and so to some extent perpetuated. Indeed, those who adjust well to marriage on the criteria usually examined are often people whose parents have been 'happily' married also.

Frequently, too, they are people whose values conform closely to those of their social groups. Furthermore it would seem likely that endogamous mating, particularly when reinforced by common interests, enhances the probability of achieving satisfactory marital adjustment, for similarities of background and interests (the two are often interdependent) lessen the chances of culture conflict situations arising. When similar backgrounds include firm religious beliefs which, whatever the denomination, tend to combine with a striving for high standards of personal conduct, the outlook is strengthened still more.

Personalities must also 'fit'. In this context the theory of complementary needs has been widely discussed. Some psychologists have maintained that complementary needs are fundamental in sex attraction. Every individual has certain needs which are closely related to his personality characteristics, and the best matches are likely to be those where the needs of the partners do not compete but are complementary. For example, a marriage between a placid, domesticated woman and a thrusting, ambitious man might work out better than one where both were ambitious or both easy-going. Complementary needs, then, are regarded by many as positive predictors of good adjustment in marriage.

It must be emphasised that all these predictors of marital success or failure are related to statistical probabilities only and that there are many individual variations. Marital adjustment is a continuous process. It is not achieved once and for all. Marriage partners can grow apart rather than together over the years and indeed it is not unlikely that they will do so, particularly beyond the child-rearing years. At the oldest age groups, age itself may have something to do with this. But in the middle years, age is not necessarily a factor, for some marriages improve in their degree of adjustment at this time and, furthermore, deteriorated marriage adjustment can be manifest without diminution of personal adjustment of the kind associated with old age.

Thus it can be seen that variations in marital adjustment are closely related to the family developmental cycle. The degree of adjustment required is greater at some stages than at others. Crises are frequent at the time of the birth of the first child when the wife's interests and energies are focused on the baby rather than on her husband, when freedom to go out is suddenly restricted, and when slender budgets may be strained to the limit. There may be other reasons too, such as lack of experience and inadequate understanding of or preparation for parenthood; many competent young women, it has been shown, suffer feelings of inadequacy as mothers, as Hannah Gavron has shown. Late middle age and the departure of the last child from home also ushers in a particularly crisis-prone period when, after the unremittingly concentrated exertion of providing for the material, emotional and social needs of the young, each of the ageing marriage partners has time to make a cool appraisal of the other as a companion for the long years ahead and to nurse dormant grievances back to life. The malaise is intensified by the indeterminate nature of cultural goals at this stage as compared with earlier clear-cut obligations to nurture and rear the young appropriately. In sum, the most crisis-prone phases of the family life cycle are those which are transitional and call for big adjustments. But all changes which may occur as the family cycle rolls on—ageing, ill health, loss of income, to mention a few—bring about different interactions and so have significance for personal relationships and family stability.

The 'success' of a marriage may be judged on criteria other than those of personal happiness to which we have directed our attention so far and for which the personality structures and general compatibility of the spouses are of central importance. Stability is sometimes viewed as synonomous with durability, and personal happiness is only one of the variables which correlate positively with stability in this sense.

Marriage, and hence the family, are likely to be stable in small communities in which primary relationships predominate over the secondary relationships that are characteristic of modern urban settings. For example, in villages in which there is an often intimate knowledge of other people's affairs, or in any homogeneous community in which there is little or no disagreement on values and standards of behaviour, deviations from the norms call forth strong sanctions. Stability of marriage is also certain when divorce is prohibited by the Church, or by law as in, for example, Spain and Italy. But it does not necessarily follow that family life in these circumstances will be harmonious, and there may be a high rate of separation.

Marriage will also be stable when the family is economically functional and thus an important unit of social organisation, or in any situation where marriage tends to be primarily an economic arrangement. Property is another traditional bond. When a dowry, bride price or trust settlement is involved, divorce is not treated lightly, particularly if the property has to be returned afterwards. Interestingly, however, if the property is portable and easily divisible, divorce becomes more common, as it did in our own country among the upper classes after the advent of limited liability made stocks and shares relatively safe and a much more convenient and flexible form in which to hold property than land or buildings. Male dominance, too, is positively correlated with stable marriage. When male authority is absolute, divorce is strongly inhibited, as at the height of 'patria potestas' in ancient Rome. Associated with marriage forms in which the motives are primarily economic rather than sexual, it has close links with property also, for men seek to impose rules limiting the freedom of women with a view to ensuring that only their own legitimate children will inherit their property. Such rules are often reinforced by religious beliefs. The Christian ethic, for example, has always stressed fidelity, and by the end of the Middle Ages marriage had become an indissoluble union. Great value was put upon love in the sense of *agape* and high ideals for personal relationships emerged. Until the present century, throughout Western Europe, the law has underwritten effectively the Church's teaching on the sanctity of marriage. But with secular values challenging the authority of the Church, marriage for many is no longer regarded as a sacrament. Secular values have modified attitudes to marriage in other ways, too. Duty to spouse, to children, to the family honour and so on, used to be emphasised much more than personal happiness, which has now become the chief criterion of successful marriage. In its ideal type, marriage in our society demands first and foremost, romantic love, together with monogamy, prenuptial chastity and marital faithfulness. Such demands within the setting of the small relatively isolated nuclear group, often with little support from an extended kingroup, put strains on marriages which are not present in some other societies where marriage has somewhat different ideals and clearer-cut goals.

It has also been forcefully argued that from a societal point of view the soundly based personal preference for endogamous marriage is divisive. It is equally arguable that if there were more socially mixed marriages but less personal satisfaction, accentuated frictions in society itself could as probably follow. Stable marriages and family life, for which personal happiness is now an important ingredient, make for cohesion in society, and for satisfaction with the *status quo*, which is one reason why political extremists have attacked them.

Widowhood and old age

Death is the one irrevocable termination of a marriage relationship, whether the wind has blown fair or foul. Always a traumatic event, widowhood is a more common experience for women than for men; in every age group there are higher proportions of women widowed than men, and in middle age nearly three times as many. This is a time of life when the widow is likely to be faced with multiple difficulties and little to look forward to. Her children are leaving the nest so that home-making ceases to provide a satisfying *raison d'être*; her training, if any, may have grown rusty, or she may, on account of health or other problems, be ill-equipped to re-enter a competitive labour market; her fading looks combined with the increasing proportion of women to men in the later age groups limit her chances of re-marriage; her social life, on a reduced income and in a society in which marriage as such still confers status on a woman, is also likely to be circumscribed. One way and another, long years stretch bleakly ahead with roles restricted and much reduced in number.

In a secular age with a declining belief in an after life, death seems more final than in the days when it was regarded merely as the end of a stage in experience, and when confidence in a reunion in happier surroundings could provide consolation. Often, too, the widow is now denied whatever solace can be derived from mourning. The practices connected with mourning vary in different cultures or sub-cultures, but whatever their nature they appear to serve functional ends. In accordance with many religious beliefs it is necessary to ease the transition of the departing soul by prayer or other means. In some societies the lengthy and elaborate ritual is designed to console the living; it provides time to rearrange property and authority, and to make provision for dependants. Sometimes there are institutionalised ways of providing for the widow. She may immediately marry her late husband's brother, a not uncommon practice in simpler societies known as the *levirate*, or she may be protected by him. Sometimes she may be treated as having no separate existence apart from her husband and be regarded as 'one flesh', as in the marriage service of the established Church and as in English law before women were emancipated. Carried to its logical conclusion this view can lead to mandatory self-destruction by the widow, for example the practice of *suttee* in India where the widow threw herself on her husband's funeral pyre.

In our own society there are fewer institutionalised ways of coping with death, grief and widowhood than in simple societies. In traditional and rural communities considerable ritual is still observed, and it marks changes of role and status which may affect a wide kingroup or even a whole community; and in these circumstances it also performs a cohesive function in the community, for everyone is expected to take part. In some strata of society, often those of the highest and the lowest, mourning is also semi-public with elaborate ceremonies attached and large gatherings of kinsmen and others, as for Irish wakes and for the funerals of national heroes or of royalty. As with weddings, great ceremonial often means that correspondingly great adjustments will have to be made by family and kin, and perhaps by the community as well if the deceased is a prominent person. Similarly the ritual serves to emphasise family or national solidarity. It enables relations to reconnoitre for pickings among the personal effects of the dead. Property has to be redistributed as in primitive societies although, except in cases of entail, the pattern of disposal is by no means uniform and not always predictable, which adds to the funeral proceedings some of the excitement of a game of chance. Funerals may even be rather jolly occasions, particularly if the deceased is 'full of years', for many families meet kin at no other times apart from weddings.

The modern matter-of-fact attitude, the curtailment of mourning, the taboo or refusal to talk about death, the feeling of inadequacy or intrusion in offering any sort of comfort, particularly without the solace of a belief in religion, leaving the body in a chapel of rest instead of at home, sending people to hospital to die, the almost unseemly haste in burying or cremating the dead; all such practices reflect an embarrassment at death, a refusal to face it, and a callous ignoring of the plight of the bereaved. The widow and children until this century probably had the consolations of religion, the support of their numerous kin and the opportunity to work through their grief in an acceptable way. It was probably with a real sense of renewal that a widow would cast off her weeds at the end of the prescribed period of mourning. For the contemporary bereaved family it is business as usual after the almost crisp obsequies. Stiff upper lips, bright colours, no outward signs; this is what society now expects. Unhappily too, in a society which demands geographical mobility from those who aspire to social mobility, the scattering of kingroups means that death for some is an experience to be faced alone, or in impersonal surroundings, particularly when it occurs in old age.

The old are not a favoured group in our society. The onset of old age is sharply heralded socially for the majority by compulsory retirement from work at an arbitrary age irrespective of physical or mental capacities; and since the coming of the welfare state with its somewhat inflexible earnings rules which inhibit pensioners from embarking on a new or part-time job, the break with the world of affairs is now more defined than in the past. Women have fewer adjustments to make than men in that the domestic roles fade as enfeeblement creeps up rather than end abruptly, but as they now assume extra-familial economic roles with increasing frequency, a generation of women, too, will shortly be facing problems of adjustment to retirement not dissimilar from those of men. However, even the wholly domestic woman is called upon to adapt when her husband has caught the five-thirty home for the last time, perhaps replete with presentation gold watch to seal the finality of the journey, and is henceforth likely to be around the house seven days a week.

Retirement is no problem in communities where the expectation of life is short; 40 is still regarded as old in some parts of the world. Nor is it a problem when the aged have functions as elders, priests or wise men. In rural, traditional or peasant economies it presents fewer or different problems than in a modern urban-industrial setting. For most in our society it is of mainly personal concern to the individual or couple affected, and is of little significance for the functioning of the community except that it leaves opportunities open to younger people (important in an achievement-conscious society), and also brings with it a responsibility for maintenance of the elderly at a time when the age structure of the population is becoming alarmingly top-heavy. Otherwise there are in the ordinary way no community interests at stake as there are when retirement means a redistribution or handing over of property as in traditional rural Ireland, or of influence and status as with the Dutch monarchy.

Virtually excluded from economic participation, a primary determinant of status as we have seen, political impotence and social isolation tend to follow, as they do not in traditional peasant family-oriented economies. The more fortunate in material terms may retire to the country or seaside house of their dreams, soon to find themselves too infirm to walk or drive to the shops or visit friends, their isolation intensified. Without roots in the neighbourhood, bereft of those who could 'drop in' and far from the bus stop, the dream becomes in reality a nightmare, the once neat garden an intolerable burden. All become poorer the longer they live, and this applies at every social level for pensions rarely keep pace with inflationary prices; the only exceptions are those who have an interested and knowledgeable person to look after their investments. But the majority have relatively fixed incomes; stocks of clothes and household goods, adequate on retirement, wear out and are often impossibly expensive to replace, and the fabric and decorative state of the house deteriorates as maintenance costs mount. Advancing age, too, leaves them open to exploitation by the unscrupulous. And, sooner or later, one will be left to cope alone.

Conclusion

Family sociology and family policy

In this book we have examined the family as an institution interacting with other institutions and as a small group of interacting personalities and we have observed the principal social influences which act upon it. Our analysis has been mainly in terms of concepts and theories which were developed and have proved fruitful in other fields of sociological endeavour. Indeed, our quest to understand the social processes underlying family behaviour has been hampered in so far as family sociology has lagged behind other branches of sociology in building an adequate body of theory. Apart from the *life developmental cycle*, still very unrefined, there is little in the way of conceptual framework or theory which is specifically *familial*. Nevertheless, we have been able to identify certain sets of inter-related propositions about the family which are beginning to approximate to theory, and *explanations* as distinct from descriptions of the processes at work, although still rudimentary, are beginning to emerge. Clearly there are many problems awaiting solution which are wholly *sociological* in character.

However, much research on the family has been triggered off by problems clamouring for investigation which are purely *social* such as the obvious urgency of many situations which arose as a consequence of the economic depression of the thirties, to give an example. In our own analysis, carefully confined to the actual not the ideal, problem situations which lead potentially to distress, tension and crisis have persistently obtruded themselves, although the text was not designed to give them prominence. They can hardly be ignored by a society in which, as we have seen, the family continues to perform important functions, and has shown its capacity, too, to adapt to the rapidly changing needs of growing industrialisation by, for example, adjusting to the demand for geographical mobility. Even experiments such as the Kibbutz can be viewed not as a repudiation of the family but as evidence that it has sufficient resilience to adopt unfamiliar forms in a changing world. All in all, a rapid disintegration of the family seems unlikely in the immediate future provided it continues to fulfil its now highly specialised functions, particularly those relating to socialisation.

In so far as performing a function creates an obligation, it is possible to argue that society has some duty to provide conditions in which the family can function with optimal efficiency and minimal trauma, and this point of view is implicit in the very existence of social policies relating to the family. Furthermore empirical evidence shows, as we have seen, that in modern Britain (and elsewhere) people attach a positive value to the family as such and to certain of its characteristics; and in a society subscribing to a democratic ethos, social policy designed to support the family may be regarded as the distillation of a societal value. Indeed, unless policies are founded on a degree of consensus, they cannot be valid in a democracy. General values which must necessarily underlie family policies in Britain have been clarified in the text. Social justice is central and finds its expression in the demand for equality of opportunity as an avenue to social mobility. But as we have seen also, there are many differing value systems within our culture which must be either exploited or reconciled if policies are to be successful. Goals must also be practicable which means that they must be related realistically to the total and changing social structure.

The link between sociology and social policy is in some respects a controversial one, but there can be few who would deny that policies rationally based on an understanding of social processes and needs are preferable to those derived from prejudices, partisan interests, misconceptions, or sentiments alone, however high-minded. Sociology can contribute some of the knowledge which goes to the making of intelligent and viable social policy. Although it can rarely supply immediately a detailed policy blueprint to fit particular situations without further investigations, sociological knowledge can confirm the existence of a need, it can provide a guide to or check on the direction of policies which are contemplated, and it can play a part in weighing up the feasibility of alternatives. Family sociology stands in this relationship to family policy-making.

Family policies are in essence directed towards promoting effective role performance. They can be classified under three main headings: rescue, for those with problems of crisis magnitude; prophylactic, with the objective of mitigating or circumventing stress-productive situations by ensuring that families have the material and emotional resources to cope with the expected strains in the 'normal' family life cycle; and lastly the 'life-enriching' policies which have the more positive goal of improving the quality of family life, and which embrace all families including those not in any sense 'at risk'. There tends to be least emphasis on the third category because of the more urgent demands of the first two. The findings of sociology are relevant to all three and, specifically, as we have noticed earlier, they clarify the processes which precipitate the tensions and crises which may precede family disorganisation and breakdown.

In so far as there now exists a theory of family disorganisation the principal variables have been identified as poverty, inadequate role performance and personal interaction, disregard or misunderstanding of societal norms, and family attitudes to the traumatic situation. We owe the systematisation of these ideas mainly, although not entirely, to Americans such as E. R. Mowrer and Reuben Hill who have sought to make explicit the sociological relevance of studies of family stress and who have identified many of the linked sequences of interdependence.

Some of the factors which provoke or intensify stress within the family, such as poverty, have been publicised for generations. Even before the turn of the century Charles Booth had presented an account of the disruptive effects of old age, ill health, the strains of urban living with its uncertainty of regular employment, low income for whatever reason, the stage in the family developmental cycle, and personal inadequacies; a formidably lengthy list. Later researchers have identified and emphasised other aspects of the family disorganisation syndrome. But income is still regarded as fundamental to material and emotional security, affected as it is by the interlocking factors of the location of the family home, the nature of local industries, the variety of employment in the area and the availability of commuter transport. All these are central to the father's role performance as provider and in turn are linked with his education and personal qualities. The standard of living attained on a given income depends, too, on the way it is laid out and thus, in many social strata, on the role adequacy of the mother as principal spender, and the limits within which she can manoeuvre the family budget are set by the stage reached in the family life cycle.

The relative significance of different factors in the aetiology of family disorganisation may be assessed tentatively as in proportion to the frequency with which they appear in different linked sequences of cause and effect. For example, the home and its location, already referred to in relation to the economic environment of the family, emerges as important in other connections. If it is situated in a delinquency-producing area its location may effectively inhibit family members from absorbing the norms acceptable in the general culture. Substandard or unsuitable housing is also known to exacerbate family tensions and to undermine marriages which in a more favourable environment might have survived. We may, therefore, hypothesise that the home and its location are of more than peripheral importance for family welfare.

Health is positively linked with good housing, it affects and is affected by income, but it also impinges on many other facets of family life. Any chronic or recurrent illness, physical disability, or mental abnormality requires a reallocation of tasks and a readjustment of familial roles and relationships both internally and externally. Tension may be a product of these adjustments and conflict may also ensue when there is resistance to the rearrangement of roles, accompanied as it must be by changes in statuses and hence in the distribution of authority also.[1]

A change in the status of the family itself is another stress-productive situation, and one in which changed roles and role expectations are involved, not always harmoniously, as a consequence of lost or altered norms.[2] An anomic situation may arise and conflict within the family become intensified also when the family is socially mobile irrespective of whether the movement is upwards or downwards. Conflicts can be associated, for example, with loss of income, with disasters such as persecution or war; or on the other hand, as Durkheim was well aware, with fame and fortune beyond the usual expectations of the individual's social group of origin, with educational attainment beyond the parental level and so on.

Both meaning and resources are important internal variables in dealing with any situation which has crisis potential.[3] The amount of stress a family experiences when difficulties arise may depend on their meaning to that family; for the same event can have a different meaning for different families. Failure to obtain a grammar-school place, for example, is likely to have a more traumatic effect on families in which the parents have already reached a grammar-school level of education than in families where the expectation of success is slight. Resources for dealing with the same event also differ. For example, if private school fees can be afforded the stress associated with 11 + selection may be less severe than if they cannot.

The extent to which resources can be effectively deployed in averting the disruptive effects of an event may depend on its source. If it is external, the family may be virtually powerless to avert it, as in the case of a pit closure. In such circumstances, which arouse sympathy and are shared by others, emotional and material resources may be harnessed in co-operative efforts to overcome the difficulty and family solidarity cemented as a consequence. But if the event is preventable, as when it is precipitated by negligence, or if it is considered to be discreditable, family relationships are likely to be injured and the stability of the family endangered.

It has been suggested so far that stressful situations and their effects are in part a function of socio-economic environment and of the attitudes induced. Personality structures as revealed in internal family relationships contribute a further dimension to the understanding of the processes involved. Family relationships are never static and because they are always in process they are sometimes elusive. As the founding and central figures of the nuclear family it follows that the personality structures of the marriage partners are of particular importance. Their compatibility, their adaptability, the maturity of their attitudes all have significance for the emotional well-being of the whole group. Good interpersonal relationships can prevent stress from turning into crisis even when physical and material resources are inadequate. Given stable, well-integrated and adaptable internal relationships, adversity can strengthen family structure in the long run, even although the short-term effects are seemingly disastrous. Whether or not the family is fortified or undermined often depends on how well it was meeting the emotional needs of its members before the onset of the crisis. It has been shown that when the usual patterns of family life break down under pressure the seeds of disintegration are usually present before the precipitating event. Families composed of anxious, neurotic personalities with inadequate role performances may regard difficulties as mountainous when in reality they possess resources adequate to shift their molehills, but they are nevertheless incapable of 'pulling themselves together' as they are so often advised, because of the meaning they attach to the situation, which is itself in part a function of their personality structures. Conversely, families who surmount stresses and crises successfully tend to have adequate role performance by each individual member of the family, each fulfils the role expectations of the others, and all are quick to adapt their roles when conditions change and tensions arise. In practical terms this means that well-organised families with good interpersonal relationships, who have prepared to meet foreseeable eventualities, adjust most easily.

It may be concluded, therefore, that adequate family policies must comprise supportive services which satisfy certain criteria. They must facilitate family adaptation to changing environmental conditions, for adaptability is essential to the survival of the family as an institution; and they must also enable family members to perform their roles well. In addition, both the goals and the means of implementing them must embody values which have wide currency in the society or social group.

References and further reading

INTRODUCTION

1. Ronald Fletcher, *The Family and Marriage*, Penguin Books, 1962, p. 16 and p. 177.

2. Edmund Leach, 'Ourselves and Others', 3rd Reith Lecture 1967, reported in *Listener*, 30.11.67.

Further reading

Norman W. Bell and Ezra F. Vogel (eds.), *A Modern Introduction to the Family* (Part I), The Free Press: Glencoe, Ill., 1968 ed.

Church of England Moral Welfare Council, *The Family in Contemporary Society*, S.P.C.K., 1958.

A. S. Makarenko, *The Collective Family: A Handbook for Russian Parents*, Anchor Books, N.Y., 1967.

M. E. Spiro, *Children of the Kibbutz*, Harvard U.P., Cambridge, Mass., 1958.

CHAPTER 1

1. Edward Westermarck, *A Short History of Marriage*, Macmillan, London, 1926, p. 1 *et seq.*

2. G. Gorer, *Exploring the English Character*, Cresset, 1955, p. 161.

3. Alex Comfort, *Sex in Society*, Penguin Books, 1962, p. 88.

4. See Chapter 7 for a detailed discussion.

Further reading

Ruth Anshen, *The Family: Its Function and Destiny*, Harper & Brothers, N.Y., 1959 ed.

E. W. Burgess and E. J. Locke, *The Family from Institution to Companionship*, The American Book Coy., N.Y., 1963 ed.

Kingsley Davis, *Human Society*, Macmillan, N.Y., 1964 ed.

W. Goodsell, *History of Marriage and the Family*, Macmillan, N.Y., 1923.

Robert F. Winch, *The Modern Family*, Holt, Reinhart and Winston, N.Y., 1963 ed.

CHAPTER 2

1. See Chapter 4.

2. Dr Eustace Chesser, 'Is Chastity Outmoded?' in *Getting Married*, Family Doctor Special, 1956, p. 41.

Further reading
W. J. Goode, *World Revolution and Family Patterns*, The Free Press: Glencoe, Ill., 1963.

George P. Murdock, *Social Structure*, Macmillan, N.Y., 1949.

W. H. Williams, *Sociology of an English Village: Gosforth*, Routledge & Kegan Paul, 1956.

W. H. Williams, *A West Country Village: Ashworthy*, Routledge & Kegan Paul, 1963.

Carl Zimmerman, *Family and Civilisation*, Harper, N.Y., 1957.

Also as for Introduction and Chapter 1.

CHAPTER 3

1. C. Rosser and C. Harris, *The Family and Social Change*, Routledge & Kegan Paul, 1965, p. 229.

2. C. Bell, 'Mobility and the Middle Class Extended Family', *Sociology*, Vol. 2, No. 2.

3. ibid.

4. Peter Townsend, 'The Four Generation Family', *New Society*, 7.7.66.

5. J. H. Goldthorpe *et al.*, 'The Affluent Worker and the Thesis of Embourgeoisement', *Sociology*, Vol. 1, No. 1 (1967).

6. P. Willmott, *The Evolution of a Community*, Routledge & Kegan Paul, 1963.

7. H. J. Gans, *The Levittowners*, Allen Lane, 1967.

Further reading

Elizabeth Bott, *Family and Social Network*, Tavistock, 1957.

R. Firth, *Family and Kinship in Industrial Societies*, Sociological Review, Monograph No. 8, 1964.

R. Firth, *Two Studies of Kinship in London*, Athlone Press, 1956.

Ruth Glass, *Newcomers*, Allen & Unwin, 1960.

H. Jennings, *Societies in the Making*, Routledge & Kegan Paul, 1960.

P. H. Mann, *An Approach to Urban Sociology*, Routledge & Kegan Paul, 1965.

J. M. Mogey, *Family and Neighbourhood*, O.U.P., 1956.

R. N. Morris and J. Mogey, *The Sociology of Housing*, Routledge & Kegan Paul, 1965.

M. Stacey, *Tradition and Change*, O.U.P., 1960.

P. Townsend, *The Family Life of Old People*, Penguin Books, 1963.

W. H. Williams, *Sociology of an English Village : Gosforth*, Routledge & Kegan Paul, 1956.

P. Willmott and M. Young, *Family and Class in a London Suburb*, Routledge & Kegan Paul, 1960.

L. Wirth, *The Ghetto*, Chicago U.P., 1928.

M. Young and P. Willmott, *Family and Kinship in East London*, Routledge & Kegan Paul, 1957.

CHAPTER 4

1. Talcott Parsons and Robert F. Bales (eds.), *Family, Socialisation and Interaction Process*, The Free Press: Glencoe, Ill., 1955.

2. See p. 23.

3. John and Elizabeth Newson, *Patterns of Infant Care in an Urban Community*, Penguin Books, 1965.
   The survey was specifically designed to discover the extent to which fathers participate in the care of their young children (up to 12 months old) and was based on 709 interviews with normally constituted families, with normal, legitimate babies, being cared for by their own mothers. On the evidence, 52 per cent of the fathers were rated as 'highly participant', meaning that they would help in any way at all; 27 per cent were rated 'moderately participant', meaning that they would do anything *if asked*, but not necessarily as a matter of course; 21 per cent were rated 'non-participant'.

4. op. cit. Only 9 per cent of middle-class mothers had any paid domestic help at all in prosperous Nottingham and half of these had it for less than six hours a week.

5. op. cit., p. 139.

6. Josephine Klein, *Samples from English Cultures*, Vol. I, Routledge & Kegan Paul, 1965, p. 110.

CHAPTER 5

1. See p. 24.

2. Among graduates with children 54 per cent are gainfully employed, 25 per cent of them full-time. Constance Arreger, *Women Graduates at Work*, The British Federation of University Women, 1965.

3. Simon Yudkin, *0–5 Report on the Care of Pre-School Children*, Allen & Unwin, 1967.

4. e.g. Yudkin and Holme found 425 out of 1650 children managed on their own after school. Figure includes 90 out of 367 in 5–11 age group. 431 out of 1650 had little or no holiday supervision, 71 out of 367 aged 5–11. When ill 41 out of 1650 were just left; 15 of these aged 5–11.
   (S. Yudkin and A. Holme, *Working Mothers and Their Children*, Michael Joseph, 1963.)

5. Barbara Wootton, 'Twelve Criminological Hypotheses', in *Social Science and Social Pathology*, Allen & Unwin, 1960.

6. Some examples are almoners, 65 per cent below the desirable strength, librarians 50 per cent below and a variety of others at least 20 per cent below. (Viola Klein, *British Journal of Sociology*, Vol. XVII, No. 2.)

7. It should be noted that some local authorities are currently cutting down teaching staffs as part of an economy drive.

8. Alva Myrdal and Viola Klein, *Women's Two Roles*, Routledge & Kegan Paul, 1956.

Further reading (Chapters 4 and 5)
M. Banton, *Roles*, Tavistock, 1965.

Norman W. Bell and Ezra W. Vogel (eds.), *A Modern Introduction to the Family* (Part III), The Free Press: Glencoe, Ill., 1968 ed.

E. Bott, *Family and Social Network*, Tavistock, 1957.

N. Dennis *et al.*, *Coal is Our Life*, Eyre & Spottiswoode, 1956.

H. Gavron, *The Captive Wife*, Routledge & Kegan Paul, 1966.

P. Jephcott, N. Seear and J. Smith, *Married Women Working*, Allen & Unwin, 1962.

Viola Klein, *Working Wives*, I.P.M., 1960.

Gordon Rose, *The Working Class*, Longmans, 1968.

James Spence *et al.*, *A Thousand Families in Newcastle-upon-Tyne*, O.U.P., 1954.

R. M. Titmuss, *Essays on the Welfare State*, Allen & Unwin, 1958.

P. Willmott and M. Young, *Family and Class in a London Suburb*, Routledge & Kegan Paul, 1960.

M. Young and P. Willmott, *Family and Kinship in East London*, Routledge & Kegan Paul, 1957.

F. Zweig, *The Worker in the Affluent Society*, Heinemann, 1961.

CHAPTER 6

1. J. W. B. Douglas and J. M. Blomfield, *Children Under Five*, Allen & Unwin, 1958.

2. J. Spence *et al.*, *A Thousand Families in Newcastle-upon-Tyne*, O.U.P., 1954, p. 120.

3. R. G. Andry, 'Paternal and Maternal Roles and Delinquency', in W.H.O., *Deprivation of Maternal Care*, Public Health Papers 14, Geneva, 1962, p. 31.

4. Mary Truby King, *Mothercraft*, Whitcombe & Tombs Ltd., 1943, p. 4.

5. ibid., p. 65.

6. ibid., p. 192.

7. Benjamin Spock, *Baby and Child Care*, The Bodley Head, 1955.

8. The term 'child-rearing' is not consistently used in the literature. In this chapter it is used to include training techniques and deliberately designed social interaction, together with the more casual contacts which arise as a consequence of the particular social milieu all of which are clearly not directed to 'training' in the narrower sense.

9. R. R. Sears, E. Maccoby and H. Levin, *Patterns of Child Rearing* (a study of 379 American-born suburban mothers of 5-year-old boys and girls), Ron Paterson & Co., N.Y., 1957.

Further reading

J. H. S. Bossard and E. S. Boll, *The Sociology of Child Development*, 4th ed., Harper and Row, N.Y., 1965.

John Bowlby, *Maternal Care and Mental Health*, W.H.O., 1951.

E. H. Erikson, *Childhood and Society*, Penguin Books, 1963.

Hilde T. Himmelweit *et al.*, *Television and the Child*, O.U.P., 1958.

D. G. McKinley, *Social Class and Family Life*, The Free Press, N.Y., 1964.

J. B. Mays, *Growing Up in the City*, Liverpool University Press, 1954.

M. Mead, 'A Cultural Anthropologist's Approach to Maternal Deprivation', in W.H.O., *Deprivation of Maternal Care*, Public Health Papers 14, Geneva, 1962.

M. Mead, *Growing Up in New Guinea*, Wm. Morrow, N.Y., 1930, and Penguin Books, 1942, 1954.

F. W. J. Miller *et al.*, *Growing Up in Newcastle-on-Tyne*, O.U.P., 1960.

E. and J. Newson, *Patterns of Infant Care in an Urban Community*, Allen & Unwin, 1963.

Talcott Parsons and Robert F. Bales, *Family, Socialization and Interaction Process*, The Free Press, N.Y., 1955.

B. M. Spinley, *The Deprived and the Privileged*, Routledge & Kegan Paul, 1953.

W. H. Whyte, *The Organisation Man*, Penguin Books, 1960.

Harriet Wilson, *Delinquency and Child Neglect*, Allen & Unwin, 1962.

D. W. Winnicot, *The Child, the Family and the Outside World*, Penguin Books, 1964.

S. Yudkin and Anthea Holme, *Working Mothers and Their Children*, Michael Joseph, 1963.

CHAPTER 7

1. i.e. those whose incomes are derived from land or other considerable property and who traditionally do not themselves work for money except marginally.

2. John and Elizabeth Newson, op. cit.
   In their Nottingham study the Newsons found that 60 per cent of mothers in social classes I and II were breast-feeding when the baby was one month old, 39 per cent at three months and 20 per cent at six months. The comparable figures for social class V (the lowest) were 34 per cent, 12 per cent and 7 per cent.

3. J. H. Goldthorpe *et al.*, op. cit.

4. These arguments are elaborated by D. G. McKinley, *Social Class and Family Life*, Free Press of Glencoe, N.Y., 1964.

5. Upper-class attitudes, traditionally oriented to uphold the family honour rather than towards personal achievement, are also becoming individualistic.

6. J. W. B. Douglas, *The Home and the School*, MacGibbon & Kee, 1964.

7. J. W. B. Douglas, op. cit.

8. David C. McClelland, 'The Urge to Achieve', *New Society*, 16.2.67.

9. J. Floud, F. Martin and A. H. Halsey, *Social Class and Educational Opportunity*, Heinemann, 1956, pp. 49–50.

10. J. W. B. Douglas, op. cit.

11. Described by Dale B. Harris, 'Values and Standards in Educational Activities', *Social Casework*, Vol. 39, Nos. 2 and 3, pp. 163–4.

Further reading

Basil Bernstein and Douglas Young, 'Social Class Differences in Conceptions and Uses of Toys', *Sociology*, Vol. 1, No. 2.

M. P. Carter, *Home, School and Work*, Pergamon, 1962.

D. V. Glass (ed.), *Social Mobility in Britain*, Routledge & Kegan Paul, 1954.

Mollie Harrington, 'Parents' Hopes and Children's Success', *New Society*, 26.11.64.

Brian Jackson and Dennis Marsden, *Education and the Working Class*, Routledge & Kegan Paul, 1962.

J. H. Kahn and J. P. Nurstein, *Unwillingly to School*, Pergamon, 1964.

Josephine Klein, *Samples from English Cultures*, vol. II., Routledge & Kegan Paul, 1965.

J. B. Mays, *Education and the Urban Child*, Liverpool University Press, 1962.

F. Musgrove, *The Family, Education and Society*, Routledge & Kegan Paul, 1966.

George Orwell, *The Road to Wigan Pier*, Penguin Books.

W. P. Robinson and S. J. Rackshaw, 'Mothers' Answers to Children's Questions', *Sociology*, Vol. 1, No. 3.

D. F. Swift, 'Social Class, Mobility–Ideology and 11+ Success', *British Journal of Sociology*, Vol. XVIII, No. 2.

D. F. Swift, 'Social Class and Achievement Motivation', *Educational Research*, Vol. VIII, No. 2.

CHAPTER 8

1. F. Ivan Nye and Felix M. Berardo, *Emerging Conceptual Frameworks in Family Analysis*, Macmillan, N.Y., 1966.

2. It seems probable that in the mid-nineteenth century girls in the more northerly European countries reached the menarche at approximately 17, although there are few records except for Norway.

3. F. Musgrove, 'Population Changes and the Status of the Young in England since the Eighteenth Century', *Sociological Review*, Vol. 11, No. 1.

4. A recent study has shown that when all other factors are held constant, the child from the secondary modern or co-educational school, who leaves at the first possible moment, starts 'dating' and kissing earlier than the grammar-school child, and on reaching the age range 17–19 is more likely to have experienced coitus. Michael Schofield, *The Sexual Behaviour of Young People*, Longmans, 1965.

5. E. M. and M. Eppel, *Adolescents and Morality*, Routledge & Kegan Paul, 1966, p. 219.

6. D. Weintraub and M. Shapiro, 'The traditional family in Israel in the process of change—crisis and continuity', *British Journal of Sociology*, Vol. XIX, No. 3.

7. D. V. Glass (ed.), Ch. XII, J. Berent, 'Social Mobility and Marriage', *Social Mobility in Britain*, Routledge & Kegan Paul, 1954.

8. G. Gorer, op. cit., pp. 83–124.

9. Illegitimate maternities have increased by more than one-third in the period 1960–66.

10. Annual Reports of the Chief Medical Officer of the Ministry of Health.

CHAPTER 9

1. Kingsley Davis, *Human Society*, Macmillan, N.Y., p. 426.

2. R. Fletcher, *Marriage and the Family*, Penguin Books, 1962, pp. 177, 181, 209.

3. O. R. McGregor, *Divorce in England*, Heinemann, 1957.

4. In Japan there has been a continuous reduction in the divorce rate from 335 per 1000 marriages in 1890 to 87 per 1000 in 1961. G. R. Leslie, *The Family in Social Context*, O.U.P., N.Y., 1967.

5. The most dramatic upward swing took place after the Second World War, from a figure of 6250 per year in 1938 to 60,254 in 1947, consequent upon not only hasty and rash wartime marriages, but also representing a back-log of petitions from couples separated by the war and, therefore, without access to the courts, some of which were possibly marriages already on the rocks before the 1937 Act widened the grounds for divorce. The annual average figure in the fifties was well under half that for 1947, but is nevertheless represented a substantial increase on the pre-war figures. The 1966 figure of 39,067 represented an increase of more than half as much again over the 1960 figure of 23,868, so in the sixties the trend has been markedly upwards. The figures given here include annulments. These form a very small proportion of the total dissolved, e.g. only 715 out of 39,067 in 1966. Source: *Registrar-General's Statistical Review of England and Wales, 1966*.

6. In the year 1931 the marriage rate per 1000 was 56·0 for batchelors and 51·7 for spinsters; the comparable rates for 1966 were 71·6 and 81·8. Source: Registrars-General.

7. Even so 59,591 children were involved in 39,067 cases in 1966 (op. cit.).

8. The number desired has been mounting since the Second World War, it should be noted, particularly among the more educated.

9. For both sexes marriage is most likely in the 20–24 age group; for first marriages, i.e. batchelors marrying spinsters, the mean age at marriage in 1966 was 24·31 years old for men and 21·88 years old for women, a marked contrast with the comparable figures of 27·26 and 24·84 immediately before the war. The most popular age for marriage in 1966 was 21 for both men and women (although the majority of marriages take place at ages other than 21). In general, too, the longer a marriage has been in existence the more likely it is to endure. If the bride is mature (over 40) and the marriage has lasted fifteen or twenty years, the chances of divorce are negligible, although a few marriages with these characteristics are dissolved each year (op. cit.).

10. More than half the babies born within 0–7 completed months of marriage are to brides under 20 (op. cit.).

Further reading (Chapters 8 and 9)
    Michael Banton, *Roles*, Tavistock, 1965.

    Howard Becker and Reuben Hill (eds.), *Family, Marriage and Parenthood*, Heath, Boston, 1954.

    R. Benedict, *Patterns of Culture*, Routledge & Kegan Paul, 1935.

    E. W. Burgess and L. S. Cottrell, Jr., *Predicting Success or Failure in Marriage*, Prentice-Hall, N.Y., 1939.

    E. W. Burgess and P. Wallin, *Engagement and Marriage*, Lippincott, Philadelphia, 1953.

    Elizabeth Douvan and Joseph Adelson, *The Adolescent Experience*, Wiley, N.Y., 1966.

    Ronald Fletcher, *The Family and Marriage*, Penguin Books, 1962.

    W. H. Goode, *After Divorce*, The Free Press: Glencoe, Ill., 1956.

    A. J. Humphries, *New Dubliners*, Routledge & Kegan Paul, 1966.

    R. K. Kelsall, *Population*, Longmans, 1967.

    P. Marris, *Widows and Their Families*, Routledge & Kegan Paul, 1958.

    D. C. Marsh, *The Changing Social Structure of England and Wales*, Routledge & Kegan Paul, 1965.

    M. Mead, *Coming of Age in Samoa*, Penguin Books, 1942.

    Cyril Smith, *Adolescence*, Longmans, 1968.

    Peter Townsend, 'The Meaning of Poverty', *British Journal of Sociology*, Vol. XIII, No. 3.

    R. C. Williamson, *Marriage and Family Relations*, Wiley, N.Y., 1966.

    Robert F. Winch, *Mate Selection*, Harper, N.Y., 1958.

    M. Wynn, *Fatherless Families*, Michael Joseph, 1964.

CONCLUSION

  1. Reuben Hill, 'Generic Features of Families Under Stress', *Social Casework*, 39, pp. 139–50.

2. ibid., p. 142.

3. ibid., p. 142.

Further reading

Reuben Hill, *Families Under Stress*, Harper & Brothers, N.Y., 1949.

T. H. Marshall, 'The Right to Welfare', *Sociological Review*, Vol. 13, No. 3.

E. R. Mowrer, *Disorganisation Personal and Social*, Lippincott, Philadelphia, 1942.

W. F. Ogburn, 'Education, Income and Family Unity', *American Journal of Sociology*, Vol. LIII, No. 6.

A. F. Philp, *Family Failure*, Faber, 1963.

T. S. Simey, *Social Science and Social Purpose*, Constable, 1968.

Index